BEFORE IT
HITS
THE FAN

BEFORE IT HITS THE FAN

Quick Communication Tips to Help You
Resolve Conflict and Reduce Stress

by Lorna McLaren

Website: www.mclarenformulatraining.com

Email: lorna@mclarenformulatraining.com

Phone: (604) 757-3732

Ordering Information: Quantity sales. Special discounts are available on multiple purchases by corporations, associations, and others.

For details, contact the "Special Sales Department" at the address above.

Before It Hits The Fan , Lorna McLaren —1st edition, 2017

www.evolveglobalpublishing.com

Book Layout: © 2017 Evolve Global Publishing

ISBN: (Paperback) 978-1-64136-639-7

ISBN: (Hardcover) 978-1-64136-640-3

ISBN-13: (Createspace)

ISBN-10: (Createspace)

ISBN: (Smashwords)

ASIN: B072N4NTHC (Amazon Kindle)

This book is available on Barnes & Noble, Kobo, Apple iBooks (digital)

FREE Bonus Training

This book includes videos, audios, and training strategies you can use to reduce conflict, alleviate stress, and improve communication.

Get it now at:

www.BeforeItHitsTheFan.com

Corporate Training / Event Speaker

www.LornaMcLaren.com

Endorsements

"The committees met in late October and compiled lists of topic and speaker suggestions for me to assemble into a complete seminar program. One of the encore speakers included on that list was **Lorna McLaren who ranked in the top 10 speaker list for both her sessions! And two top 10 performances are even more impressive when noted that there were 189 speaker sessions on that list!!"**

Michelle Gaston, Director Professional Development
OFA Short Course, Columbus, Ohio

"The excitement in the room was obvious. Lorna McLaren, you did an amazing job of educating and entertaining this huge group! As a result, we have invited you back to speak at another conference 6 months from now in Atlantic City. **We have never invited a speaker back so quickly as we have with you."**

Margaret O'Neal, Director of Education & Certification
Pennsylvania Landscape & Nursery Association

"Four of us from the Eisenhower Medical Center came to a conference in Palm Springs. We were blown away by one of the speakers, Lorna McLaren. We laughed, we related, and we learned so many tips on handling conflict, personality styles and how to communicate with diplomacy. Never

laughed and learned so much at a training event before. It wasn't a day about boring theory. She was spot on in knowing the stress administrators go through in various industries and what to do about it. Right then and there we new we wanted to bring her in to speak at our event. We have an annual Administrative Professional's Day Luncheon for about 85 admin staff and we've never had a speaker come before. Our COO and CNO are very progressive when it comes to the secretaries of the hospital and outside clinics. They were happy to agree to bring Lorna in. Everyone loved the program! Her humor, energy, and sincere desire to be of service shows. It was engaging, inspirational, informative and fun! We were elated when we received numerous positive responses from our Admin Staff about Lorna's presentation."

Sharon Skasick, Executive Secretary,
Administration, Eisenhower Medical Center
39000 Bob Hope Drive, Rancho Mirage, CA

"We've had the pleasure of having Lorna McLaren speak at our annual Judicial Case Managers Conference. The feedback was extremely positive. Everyone thoroughly enjoyed the topic and especially Lorna's unique presentation style. She was dynamic, entertaining, and kept everyone fully engaged the entire time!

She was right on the mark when it came to tailoring her presentation to the audience.

- *Never been as riveted by a conference speaker as I was by Ms McLaren*

- *Extremely entertaining – the best we've had yet*
- *Very captivating, refreshing and extremely interesting!*
- *A few of us needed to go to the bathroom but instead chose to stay. We didn't want to miss a thing!*
- *Really enjoyed figuring out our personalities to help me understand myself and others better*

We look forward to having you back."

Yvonne Hadfield, JCM Supervisor Office
of the Chief Judge, Vancouver, Canada

"Of the yearly training that we provide, I have never heard so many amazing comments on your delivery! Everyone was really excited and said it was their best sessions ever. Lorna, you absolutely nailed it in teaching Communication for Customer Service and Sales. Thanks!"

Lawrence Yakielashek, General Manager,
FarmLink Marketing Solutions, Canada

"Lorna, I have never been a fan of going to seminars. I always find them drab. You have changed my mind, thank you so much. You have Rocked my world"

Martin W. Brown, Sales Manager,
Edinburgh, Scotland
HSBC GLOBAL FUND SERVICES LTD

"The Conference was a truly empowering experience for me and I gained many new skills. These included; how to more effectively communicate with my boss and how to keep my boss updated on the current state of play. The

communication skills were especially useful and productive and I am still using the skills I learned from Lorna. I especially liked Lorna McLaren's teaching methods. She gave so much information which we were able to absorb because it was delivered in a very humorous way. Her manner was so caring and comfortable and she also came across as a total professional! This is a winning combination. Her mastery of the material was truly impressive!"

Maureen Regan, Economist Federal
Treasury, Canberra, Australia

"I worked with Lorna for five years as a trainer in multiple countries in front of thousands of people. Wherever Lorna went, she captivated her audience — making them think, laugh and ready to take the next step on their journey. I learned so much from Lorna and can confidently recommend her as the go-to expert in better communication and less stress."

Dr. Trina Read, Best selling author
International award winning speaker

"I want to state my deep appreciation for the tremendous positive impact you and your course had on my day to day activities this year. Thank you!!!

The positive impact you had was as follows:

First: *I appreciated the positive energy of your presentation. At first I thought "I have never seen such a clever and energetic combination of Dr. Stephen Covey, Tony Robbins & Nicholas Boothman all put together in one person (this IS a compliment)*

Second: I noticed that you broke the material down in a way that was easy to follow, with the appropriate gems.

Third: You kick started my quest for growth. I used to consider myself very much as a bit of a visionary, until I got too comfortable – and the growing stopped. I did ok, but it was not good enough. Once again, through your presentation, I realized I can and must do better. This is what I am grateful to you for. Thank you"

NICAN ELECTRICAL CONSULTING LTD.
R.A., P. Eng., Alberta, Canada

"We contacted Lorna after two of our program consultants raved about how great she was.

There were a number of things that impressed me about Lorna McLaren and her presentation style. She definitely has **an abundance of energy and approached the whole day with great enthusiasm and a willingness to do whatever was needed to make the day a success for us and the participants.** She had researched our program ahead of time, asked questions regarding all the workshop participants, and was open to any requests or suggestions we had regarding the topics she was going to address. She was very clear that she wanted to meet our expectations and provide a workshop that was worthwhile for all involved.

Lorna had based her agenda for the workshop on our requested topics but **because of her skill set was able to be very flexible in addressing situations or issues as they arose throughout the day.** She even checked in with me part way through the day to see if anything had come up that she should incorporate for the afternoon session; we discussed a few things that she easily addressed within the context of her presentation.

She was clearly a very skilled presenter as she **flowed from one topic to another responding to questions with no difficulty or hesitation**. She was funny and entertaining while still imparting very valuable and applicable information, which was noted often in her evaluations.

Lorna's manner was very easy going and light-hearted, and it was obvious that the audience enjoyed her sense of humour and appreciated her perspective. **She provided concrete and practical ideas for improving communication and interpersonal relationships, and consistently referred back to many of the key points as she moved through the day.**

Her suggestions and recommendations all had clear rationale to back them and she used many personal examples to further explain or enhance the information she was sharing. We now have tons of practical information we can draw from as well as ongoing updates through Lorna's sharing of her communication tips.

We were **definitely thrilled to have Lorna as our presenter – extremely worthwhile for all the participants in maintaining and building ongoing strong relationships, both personal and professional.** Based on our very positive experience and because her topics are so universal and she is so skilled at adapting *to any given situation, I have absolutely no hesitation in recommending Lorna for any group or organization from the social service sector to the corporate sector."*

Beth Carter, Regional Coordinator
East Kootenay Supported Child Development Program

Table of Contents

Introduction

Thank you for picking up this book. My hope is that these tips help you as much as they have helped me and thousands of others in handling communication and conflict. In the 15 plus years I've been in the corporate training arena, these are the tips that thousands of participants have told me are their favourites. They are easy to remember, easy to implement, and they work.

It doesn't matter what industry you work in; we are all people who have more in common than not. This is how to get a sense of control during conflict so it doesn't get out of control. Or worse, allow a conflict to go under the surface to feed and grow in silence.

We spend more time at work than almost any other activity on the planet. We already have enough stress going on in our lives. The intent in this book is to take away much of your stress with quick tips on what to do in the moment. We may not always be prepared for conflict. These are simple adjustments that are easy to incorporate. You will feel a positive reaction as a result of implementing them in any array of conflict situations.

The best answer for any question is "It depends." So to be on the safe side, consider these tips as rescue devices so you can't make it worse.

Before it hits the fan implies you are in a place where conflict has the potential of getting worse. It is in this moment that these tips are designed for. They also work to preempt a potential conflict long before, so it doesn't get close to the fan in the first place.

You'll find lots of quick tips to de-stress, as well as how to tap into your intelligence when the pressure gets intense or the situation seems insane. There are examples and stories on how to use these tips to get your brain churning on future applications. I toyed with the idea of giving a "thumbs up" to the author Douglas Adams (Hitchhiker's Guide to the Galaxy) by putting a "Don't Panic" button on the cover of this book.

People are amazing and we are supposed to be different. I've met so many people in various professions from small businesses to Fortune 500 corporations over 3 continents at training and conference events. Even if we are located in the same building, we are working with the globe. Any difference can cause a misunderstanding that can turn into a conflict if left uncommunicated. Most people I meet are high functioning professionals looking to be able to handle conflict better. Some are in toxic situations as a result of conflict left to grow. Most of us have worked with a chronically impossible person. Chronic means never-ending! Let's figure out how to communicate before it gets to this stage.

The most insidious and invisible damage about conflict (that is not diplomatically addressed) is in those who give up inside. Silence and resentment is a dangerous poison in any organization.

We have so many generations in our workforce. Let's face it: No matter what generation you are born in, you'll spend most of your life overcoming the first 15 years of them (ha ha). The real world awaits. Many of us were not taught how to communicate through conflict.

I know in our upbringing we were taught to ignore conflict. Don't address it. Never bring up the uncomfortable conversation or topic. It was bad manners. We would be labeled rude, wrong, and disrespectful to not agree with authority. What would people think? This was not uncommon in our generation.

Like many, I've struggled with learning how to handle conflict and communicate through difficult situations that are emotionally charged. This is the result of so many books I've read, so many people I've learned from, experiences had, gut instincts listened to, and the many crash and burns. There is no problem you can't learn yourself out of. This is a compilation of things I've learned from many venues and laced it with a perspective of levity and humour. No matter what your work environment, anytime we can better handle conflict and reduce stress is a good investment that pays huge returns.

**"Effective communication is
a thinking person's sport."**

— L. McLaren

I'm a first generation Canadian who was weaned on Bugs Bunny and went through puberty with Monty Python and Fawlty Towers. We had a British - Scottish upbringing and raised with the Canadian self deprecating attitude. We start every sentence with an apology and serve sarcasm for sport. My training style and humour is not for everyone. Fast, fun, and focused is the intent. Humour is one of the fastest ways to learn and to reduce stress.

Apparently our attention span is now one second shorter than a goldfish. Many of us have A.D. "Oh look, squirrel!" If you don't have the time or inclination to read lots of theory about conflict and just want some quick tips you can use instantly? This book is for you. Check out www.BeforeItHitsTheFan.com to get more tips, videos, and audios of this book if you are not into reading.

Changing how we think changes everything. I want to change our thoughts around conflict so it doesn't have to be a bad thing and avoided with angst. Let's embrace it! Conflict will never go away. We've all had enough bad stuff happen to us in our lives that we need some wins! If anything in this book helps you get a "win" in handling conflict with calm diplomacy, then you've made my day!

When you have a hobby or sport you love, everything about it becomes interesting. Think of conflict resolution and stress reduction as a sport or new hobby you can get better at. You'll get less bruised metaphorically speaking. I'm thankful to be able to relate to many of the communication problems you are experiencing. It can make you better. Like that quote someone said about the wheel of life either grinding you down or sharpening you up.

Having worked in unions, private sector, volunteer organizations, government contracts, owning an international business, teaching diploma programs in a college, then starting my own training business, I have learned a thing or two about conflict. In working with numerous managers and leaders, I know what your nightmares are. Frontline people, administrators, sales, IT, or anyone working with customers, I know your pain. Anyone in a family knows a thing or two about conflict, haha. We can't be silent. We need to have a voice.

"We must always take sides. Neutrality helps the oppressor, never the victim. Silence encourages the tormentor, never the tormented."
— Elie Wiesel, 1923-2016

If anything in this book helps you stand up to a bully, clarify a misunderstanding, clear the air to improve relationships, makes you feel better about yourself and the world around you then that is a win. Every person in the organization has an impact on the whole team. I don't know why they call communication a soft skill. I believe effective and respectful communication it is one of the most important skills to have of all.

The older I get, the more forgiving I am becoming. All of us are difficult when stressed. All of us are difficult when we are struggling with self esteem issues. I've lost family members at a young age. I've been in toxic work environments. I am now losing good friends to early deaths. Our time on this earth is precious and you deserve to be happy and have a voice. I have spent years regretting what I didn't do when I needed to stand up and say something all because I didn't know how to handle conflict. I'm still learning and am so much happier, fulfilled, motivated and grateful.

The best way to learn something is to teach it. I think this is why I have finally found something that gets me so excited and happy when I get to work. I get to tap into something magical when I have the opportunity to work with people in the areas of effective communication, conflict resolution, and stress reduction. None of us are successful without the support of others.

It is a newfound freedom to feel comfortable, more confident and capable in handling challenging conversations. To reduce misunderstandings and have better relationships in all areas of life as a result is wonderful. To speak with impact and diplomacy, even in the thick of a conflict is pretty cool.

Acknowledgements

Thank you my sons Lukas and Kyle for your belief in me, unlimited hugs, and for being who you are. It was such a joy raising you both! I had no idea I would appreciate it so much! You inspire me to be a better person, brought so much love, laughter, and gratitude for life into my world. The memories I have are forever savoured. My life is better because you are both in it. I feel joy when I see how you have respect for others, are self sufficient with a strong work ethic, and display an appreciation and gratitude for life. Hope I don't embarrass you too much with this book:)

Thank you to all my wonderful clients and participants at the conferences and in-house training events. It is an absolute honour and a privilege to be of service! I've had the opportunity to work with so many amazing teams and organizations on three continents. Truly impressed by the diversity, dynamics and camaraderie of the people I meet. I appreciate your kind words, sharing your trials and tribulations, and letting me know what tips worked. Especially loved hearing how you adapted them to your unique lifestyles, situations, and comfort zone. You inspire me! Thank you for suggesting, and motivating me to write this book. Sorry it took me so long . . .

My dear friend Sarah Mallinson. You were going to write the foreword to this book. You are a part of this and not a day goes by that I don't think of conversations with you in my head. You left us near Christmas and I miss you. You are the first close friend I've lost to a disease. I've seen you embrace new careers and excel in every challenge you take on. Bold, British, decisive, enthusiastic and you'll call 'Bollocks" in a heartbeat if you feel it. I admire your guts and initiative. Your support and strength has been immeasurable. You are a driving force behind getting this book done. I might worry if my humour insults in this book. Sarah would say "Bollocks" to that. So it is with joy and guts I worry not about being a safe, polite Canadian in this book. Oye!

My friend Shannon Meyer. We've gone from keeping up on the ski slopes to keeping up with the conversations and the exhilarating turns life throws in our 20 plus year friendship. What adventures we've had! Thank you for the epiphanies on the chairlift, your supportive ear, and the belly laughs when "it's just too much" life's events. Quick wit, commendable character, and instantly likeable. You are a valued sounding board and I'm lucky to have you as my friend.

Acknowledgements

The most impactful mentor, Mr. Joel Roberts. You are a riveting communication expert, engaging rapport artist, and a true master in the language of impact. Incredibly smart, savvy, and every minute I spent learning over the years at the live events et al rocked my world in so many ways! You are a genius and generous in your desire to impart your unique wisdom. Thank you for sharing your knowledge and Heidi with us. The caliber of the people you both are and how you impact those you work with is forever imprinted in my thoughts of gratitude. You are part of my DNA now. Can I get a witness:).

Thank you to all the mentors and people in my life who have helped me to believe in myself, to learn, and to grow. I have a huge appreciation and gratitude for you all. If I can be supportive, teach and be of service to others then what an amazing life this is!

Conflict Happens

When it comes to conflict, many of us don't know how to competently handle these conversations. We fear making it worse or avoid it, thus making it worse.

By learning some quick tips on how to communicate with diplomacy, you can reduce stress and resolve conflict with confidence!

This book has quick communication tips with short stories and examples on how to use them.

Conflict can start with something as simple as a misunderstanding. Misunderstandings left unchecked can ruin businesses, marriages, relationships, and be the difference between life and death. Mismanaged conflict or conflict that is not addressed with respect can poison the morale of your company. Stress is the number one killer out there!

So yeah, let's be over dramatic for a moment because it is a very real problem out there.

In my business, I meet so many people who are going through the same issues when it comes to managing conflict and reducing stress. It has been proven that diversity increases productivity, creativity, and profits. Yet with diversity comes misunderstandings. Diversity can mean so many things.

We need to have tools to address conflict with diplomacy, respect, and recovery.

People in leadership are not sure how to give negative feedback or address performance issues if they fear the employee has a high conflict status. Administrators are the communication liaisons between all the bosses, customers, and colleagues, and have no job description other than, "All duties as assigned." They become the VP's of everything, part-time therapists for their stressed out colleagues, and are struggling with managing conflict on multiple levels. IT people dealing with the 'end users' on those customer service calls struggle dealing with conflict and the high emotions of someone who doesn't understand the technology they have purchased. "There is no crying in IT!" Shy, reserved, introverted people may be inclined to hide from conflict. Some people bring conflict up in a heartbeat then forget about it instantly after. It's like they finished a sneeze and are done, while the other person labours over feelings of ill will for days as a result.

People are afraid of how to properly handle conflict. They fear being fired, reprimanded, considered "difficult", or fear the unknown of how the relationship will change if conflict is addressed.

Most of us have enough stress we just don't want to make it worse.

Don't overwhelm about conflict in general. Instead, here are some quick tips you can use right away to better react to and handle conflict while reducing stress.

All of us are difficult when stressed. All of us are difficult when struggling with self esteem issues. When someone is pointing an accusing finger at you, maybe it is because they are hurting three times more themselves. Or maybe they are just an ___.

We all have emotions, feelings, and fears that get magnified during conflict. Most difficult people don't think they are difficult at all. Let's agree that the only thing normal for sure is the setting on a washing machine.

Welcome to *Before it Hits the Fan*. It is my sincere desire you use and enjoy these tips on how to Master the Moment when it comes to communication, stress, and the Human Factor.

Be sure to check out www.BeforeItHitsTheFan.com to access more tips.

Perceive ~ Feel ~ Act

When it comes to communication and the Human Factor, be aware of this basic rule of 3.

Always these 3 things and always in this order.

How we:

- **Perceive** something determines how we
- **Feel** about it. How we feel about it determines how we
- **Act** on it.

Perceive

You've heard the phrase "Perception is reality." Or "Your perception is your reality."

It all starts with perception.

Of course, "How" we perceive things depends on many factors. A few of those factors would be our generation, gender, culture, communication style, personality trait, life experiences. When people are different, they may be wrongly perceived as being difficult, or misunderstandings happen. If you were raised in a culture that is reserved, introverted, and physical touch is rare, you may perceive someone who gives you a kiss on the cheek, or shake your hand at an introduction to be rude.

While teaching public speaking tips to a group of entrepreneurs, we got to the topic of eye contact and how to use it to engage an audience. One woman had some concerns. She stressed that in her culture, it would be a sign of disrespect to look the elders directly in the eyes when she does her presentations.

The best answer is: "It depends."

Aside from the differences of perception mentioned above, throw on top of all that things like mood, stress levels, self-esteem, prior history with the person, who has what level of authority. In conflict, if one person is in a position to fire the other, the perception and playing field changes. It definitely ups the stress level perception for the one with less control and authority.

Our moods matter in how we perceive things. If your day has been great, you may feel only a fleeting touch of frustration when someone interrupts you. If your day has been stressful, you're exhausted, rush hour traffic was insane, you'll feel your heart rate ramp-up when interrupted.

Feel

Having feelings and emotions is what makes us human! Sometimes we know why we feel a certain way. Sometimes we don't have a clue what may have triggered us to feel a certain way. We've all had those formative years and thus many underlying subconscious habits and triggers.

Driving home the point here that feelings matter!

Pick up an awareness of how feelings have an impact even if we don't know or understand why someone feels a particular way.

I remember being brought into a company to cover leadership skills training. The new owner of the company realized the management team had never had any training or consistent strategies in how to motivate, delegate, coach, prioritize, and give feedback. The corporate culture of the previous owner was, "Hey, you are our star employee! We want to promote you to management. We'll have you manage these other people. We'll give you a dollar and hour more. Good luck!"

Being good at your job is fantastic and makes you a stellar role model! Yet having experience being good at your job doesn't necessarily mean you know how to lead and manage other people to be good at their job. It's a whole different mindset and skill set. I may have had experience being a baby, doesn't mean I know how to raise one. There is a bit of a learning curve. The new owner had capable people with immeasurable experience.

"What if you don't train your employees and they stay?"

Derek Curtis Bok, the former president of Harvard University.

Most of the management team were thrilled the new owner was providing training and support to help them excel! However, there was one manager who didn't want to be taking management training. The owner gave me a heads up that the training was mandatory and not to take it personally if this particular gentleman had a bad attitude or didn't engage during the event. His perception and feelings about the training was different from the others. Old school kind of guy, he had been working at the company for 20 plus years, he knew it all. He perceived the training with resentment and as a waste of time.

And hey, I'm not saying he's wrong. Who hasn't been to a training event that was a waste of time?!? It happens. I'm sure we've all had our fill of boring, irrelevant, death by PowerPoint, painfully boring or prima donna trainers. His many years of experience without a doubt is valuable! Yet his cultural up-bringing, age, gender, professional level and ego triggered a perception of the company having doubt in his ability. To him, being forced into a course on how to do a job he's done for years implied a lack of respect to everything he has done for the company. Fair enough, we all have our perspectives.

So it was no surprise on training day that he sat at the very back of the room. His arms were crossed. He was leaning as far away as physically possible from the table in front of him. He had a look of disdain, boredom and irritation on his face. Clearly he was very put out having to be there. Yet he was there and he was looking at me. All good so far. Perhaps from his perspective he is the subject matter expert in his line of work, not some corporate trainer coming in for the day. Can't disagree with him thinking along those lines. From his perspective, he resents that he has work piling up while he is forced to be in a training event. Yep, pretty much. It doesn't have to be about agreeing or disagreeing with someone's perspective. It's about being aware of it, being empathetic and then step into it. Empathy doesn't mean you have to agree. It's about being able to see it from the other person's perspective.

The training topic was "Building a High Performing Team." As soon the subject of 'feelings' came up, I saw him roll his eyes up. He took a big audible breath, let it out, then glued his eyes to the floor. Clearly there is a perception trigger to how he perceives this topic of feelings to go. If I ignore this perception, whether I understand what it is or not, I lose him.

The owner had told me this man was dedicated, capable, respects authority and puts value on credibility. This seemed the perfect time to connect to him from a perspective he would respect and appreciate.

When it comes to managing others and the importance of feelings, allow me to reference a world renowned expert and super smart guy - Dr. Edward De Bono. De Bono is a master of applied thinking. He was nominated for a Nobel Prize and was ranked one of the Top 50 Global Thinkers which included Bill Gates, Steve Jobs, Alan Greenspan, Tom Peters, Richard Branson.

One of his many brilliant books is "The 6 Thinking Hats." He basically compartmentalizes how to think, explains the mastery behind why each category was chosen, and how to best leverage the ability to think in each category to make the best decision. One of the hats, the Red Hat, is specifically dedicated to emotions, feelings, and intuition.

Emotions give relevance to our thinking. Emotions are a driving force in building a high performing team. There is much to be lost by ignoring or condemning the importance of feelings.

Now he can relate to being open to listening to how emotions impact a team. He's gone from a perspective of tuning out to tuning in. Don't be afraid of someone's disagreement. Step into it, respect it, and go on.

The beauty of what we are talking about is this. Once you understand how someone perceives something, you can focus on communicating to how they feel about it. Or change how they feel about it by changing their perception. The focus is on them.

This works both ways. If I choose to take it personally how I perceive his actions of tuning out in a training event, I will compromise my ability to do my job well. It's not about me. That is an ego distraction that would create another conflict. Focus on them and the goal that needs to be achieved.

We yearn to feel heard and understood.

About 10 years after high school, I bumped into two women. Neither of us had seen each other in years. One eagerly shared "I'm married with two kids, pregnant again, how about you, ladies?" I mentioned I was recently engaged and that we were looking forward to starting a family. Our third friend shared that she had been married right out of high school. They have been trying so hard to start a family. She has had three miscarriages. Her voice cracked just a little bit. You could clearly hear the emotion so close to the surface even though she was stoically trying to sound calm.

The first woman said, "At least you can get pregnant. You'll be fine. I'm sure you'll have a baby in no time." Ouch! Perhaps she meant well and simply wanted to make her feel better, or give her a sense of hope by saying something positive. Perhaps she was the one so uncomfortable hearing about the miscarriage that for her comfort level she chose to ignore it.

By ignoring the gravity of what someone says or how they feel does not reduce conflict.

Just by acknowledging , "I'm so sorry to hear that. That must be devastating." Shows you were listening. It honours someone when you truly listen to them.

My dear friend Sarah comes to mind. She had never gone through the death of a friend or family member and there she was, the one who was dying. She had been cancer free for years, then it came back with a vengeance. Her family flew overseas to say goodbye, she had little time left, then she got the news she was accepted for an experimental drug. She went from a death bed to getting better. Everyone was so excited yet Sarah has always been a realist. She could talk to me about how she truly felt about dying, life, her daughter, and not being long for this world. When she tried to talk of this to others, they felt compelled to make her feel better and focus on how she can get better. It meant the world to me to have her tell me how much she appreciated being able to say anything to me and just be heard. No matter how difficult is was what she was going through or how difficult it was to hear it. I probably would have been like everyone else trying to cheer her up except that

I had been through the death of a few close family members. I knew through experience how we need to feel heard without judgement or trying to "fix" it.

Feeling heard, feeling acknowledged, feeling respected has a direct and positive impact on how we act and react.

ACT

When pulled into conflict, it is normal to fret about how the other will act or respond. So what can you control? Focus your awareness on how that person will perceive and feel as a result of how you communicate to them.

Of course you can't possibly know how everyone will perceive, feel or act about any particular topic. At a minimum, creating an environment of respect can help reduce conflict. There is a lot to be said about good manners.

Here is an example:

Let's say you notice someone carrying boxes from one room to the next. Out of the goodness of your heart, you hold the door open for them while they move their things back and forth. Let's pretend during that time and after that time, they don't acknowledge you. They don't say thank you, they don't even look at you. They treat you like some invisible gnat. How are you going to feel? Are you going to open the door for them again?

It depends.

It's possible an assertive person will let them know a thank you would be appreciated. Or maybe next time they don't take the initiative to hold the door open in the first place.

An aggressive person with a splash of anger issues may make a point of closing, blocking, or slamming the door.

The passive aggressive person will hold the door open then put their foot out as if trying to trip them. If you listen carefully enough, you may hear them say under their breath, "Watch your step, darling."

A passive person who tries to please everyone, worries what others will think of them, and avoids all conflict will apologize for being in the way.

Someone with low self-esteem or the martyr mentality will lay down in front of the door and have that person walk all over them on the way out.

No matter who you are, if you hold the door open for someone and they say 'Thank you", you'll probably hold it open for them again. So at a minimum, create an environment of respect and appreciation. Use respectful words, respectful tone, and respectful body language.

People don't care how much you know until they know how much you care

-Joe Manchin

Just by action of allowing them to say it out loud helps get the stress out. It's common in friendship. They complain to you about their situation. You ask, "What can I do to help?" And they say "Nothing, I just wanted to get it off my chest."

Have you ever had a customer very upset on the phone, speaking with anger and not letting you get a word in? And has it ever happened to you when the customer vents and you treat them with respect, after getting rid of their stress, they actually apologize for their behaviour? They can think more clearly when they have reduced the pressure of stress. By you allowing them to feel heard, allowed them to act more respectfully towards you.

www.BeforeItHitsTheFan.com to access more tips.

Communicating in 3V

The Impact of Verbal, Vocal, and Visual:

Verbal: words, semantics
Vocal: tone, pitch, speed, cadence, volume
Visual: non-verbal, body language

When conflict is at your door, to help reduce it, and/or be able to preempt it from getting worse, be aware of the impact of each of the 3Vs of communication. Your words, tone, and body language has an instant and direct impact on how that person is going to feel. And it all happens so fast, especially during an impromptu conflict.

There you are just doing your job and then **BLAM!**

An irate customer who you've never met calls you upset about something you had nothing to do with.

You're walking to the staff room and then **POW!**

A colleague corners you about a problem they've been thinking about for days and are now fully primed to bring it up!

You finish a successful meeting, keen to get started on a new project and then **WHAM!**

One of your subordinates takes personal insult to a team member, big personality clash, and wants you to intervene NOW and be on their side!

You delegate a job to someone and then **SPLAT!**

You realize they have done it so wrong, it will now take you 10 times longer to do it yourself! The client is on their way now to talk to you about it and they are livid. You feel your own emotions and sense of angst going up. You need to be the consummate professional at this impromptu meeting happening in mere moments.

What do you do when the conflict is here, the pressure is high, and the moments are brief?

What do you say in that defining moment? How do you say it when your emotions are starting to take over? You don't want to make your day-to-day relationship with a co-worker worse!

"In life as in chess, forethought wins."

- Charles Buxton

T'is true. Sage advice to think and plan in advance. Yet this particular book is about Quick Tips you can easily remember and implement "in the moment." It is for when you don't have the time, ability, inclination, or awareness to prepare for each particular conflict.

If you remember these 3V tips and give them a try, you'll be quickly surprised at how easy and effective they can be. You may already be very aware of them yet a slightly different perspective can 're-shuffle the deck' on how we see everything in general.

The intent is to be aware of all three of these areas of communication and how each has a direct impact on how we feel and how our communication is perceived. We can gain a sense of control in how the communication environment is created and how to get it back to a respectful environment. We can have a direct impact in reducing the stress during communications of conflict. The more you practice it, the easier the new habit forms. So at a minimum, during conflict remember and try these tips. Hopefully it is easy to remember!

3V almost sounds like 3D. Kind of catchy.

From a visual standpoint, a peace sign kind of looks like the letter V.

You'll have more peace in communicating with others if you remember the 3V's.

Verbal

Words have an impact on how we perceive things. Words get the brain thinking in a particular way. We may visualize images or infer meaning based on the words we use and hear.

If you were to say to your children, "Don't have a messy room." What are you visualizing? "I won't let them make me cry." What are you visualizing and to whom have you given control? "Whatever you do, don't visualize the American president in a pink Speedo." Does the brain visualize the word don't? No, it doesn't.

The brain goes to the words you use. It is similar to those times when you are passing someone (skiing, rollerblading, running) and you say "On your left." To warn them you are passing on their left side. Do you ever notice that person goes left a tiny bit or hesitates for just a flash before moving to their right?

To reduce conflict and stress, consider using the words of what you want to have happen, not what you don't want to have happen. A manager recounted an experience when initiating a challenging conversation with an upset subordinate. He started the conversation by stating, "Now don't get defensive, but we need to talk." The moment those words came out, the other man took on a very defensive stance and attitude.

Trigger Words

There are certain words known to be "trigger words." When things are calm and fine, these words may not bother us. Yet during conflict when emotions, pressure, and stress are heightened, these words may "trigger" an emotional reaction. Like the straw that breaks the camel's back.

So to avoid triggering more conflict and stress, be hyper diligent in the words you use and consider avoiding using these ones. Of course these words may not trigger everyone; we are different. Yet for the purpose of diplomacy, you can't go wrong by avoiding them to be on the safe side. These little gems could make a huge difference in not escalating a conflict.

Trigger #1: Why

The brain comes up with the answers of what you ask of it.

Sometimes when we hear the word "why" it triggers, "I'm being blamed, I'm being accused, and I have to defend myself." Instead, consider using the word "How." When we hear the word how, it softens it, and instead triggers the reasoning or rationale behind it.

"Why was the report late?" Gasp, defensiveness, blame trigger

"How is it that the report came in late?" Oh, let me explain how that happened.

Do you feel a difference? One triggers defensiveness, the other triggers the reasoning behind it. Or how about this…

Swap out one word and the whole context changes

"Why did you come here today and why did you wear that outfit?"

This may trigger the response, "Piss off, that's why!"

"How did you come to the decision to be here today?"

"Oh, let me explain how that happened" Takes away the blame/accusation trigger.

I met a foreman in a huge construction company where I was training on effective communication. He said their company had grown so fast, they kept promoting the laboring guys who were good at their job without teaching them how to communicate to lead others to be good at their jobs. Now 10 years later, they have this "old school style" of a bunch of guys yelling at everyone.

One particularly cantankerous guy who seems to thrive on conflict called the foreman during the break in the training seminar. The foreman said the impact was immediate when he avoided using the word why. The conversation was 50% shorter with 50% less anger as this guy wasn't as triggered. Try it!

Swap out the word "Why" and replace it with the word "How."

Trigger #2: But, Except, However

When you give someone a compliment, the moment you follow it with "but, except, however" you've now negated the compliment and thrown it back in their face. You come across as being insincere or passive aggressive.

"Nice job yesterday but… "

"Great presentation except…"

"I care about what you have to say, however…"

But out those buts! The best thing to do is to have a period or a pause after the complement. Then bring up the critique in a new sentence.

"I know you see it this way, but I see it differently."
   BAM back-slap trigger!

"I know you see it this way. I see it differently." Ever so subtle. It feels different, doesn't it? It feels more respectful, and less combative.

I remember seeing this one gentleman's mouth just drop with an epiphany spark in his eyes when he heard this. English was his third language. He said, "Oh my goodness! I say however all the time! I had no idea the effect I may be having on my customer's first impression. I send them a welcoming email stating, "Thank you for doing business with us however, we need you to fill out the client welcoming form." What a difference when you take out the "however"!

> "Thank you for doing business with us. We need you to fill out the client welcoming form."

Don't get me wrong. I'm not saying never say "but." There are times when it is appropriate, or during positive and relaxed communication where it may not trigger stress.

Actually, if you say the critique first and then say "but" it now has a positive effect of softening the critique and focusing more on the positive.

> "You took ownership and apologized, but you messed up the deal." **Ouch!**

> "You messed up the deal, but you took ownership and apologized." **Redeemed!**

Hmm, that feels noble somehow. Now during a heated argument, which phrase do you think will go over better?

It's not an easy habit to break. So here's how you cheat if you find yourself about to say the word "but" after an acknowledgement or a compliment. You could safely use the word "and" as a segue between a positive and a negative in a sentence.

"I know you see it this way, and I see it differently"
     Friendlier, more camaraderie.

These 3 sentences feel different:

"I care about what you have to say but…"

"I care about what you have to say and…"

"I care about what you have to say."

Who would you rather listen to, especially during conflict?

Some people find using the word, "yet" can also be a safe substitute for the word, but.

"I know you see it this way, but I see it differently."

"I know you see it this way, yet I see it differently."

But Out Those Buts

But beware. This is a hard habit to break! You'd be amazed how unaware we are of how often we say the word but!

Gotta say I love meeting so many different types of people in various professions or work environments when I'm doing onsite training. One particular group was a highly competitive, go-getter type. You could tell they respected each other, worked well as a team, mostly extroverted with a sense of fun was the culture of this organization. One of the managers, Wendy and I were mentioning how quickly you become aware of, and change a habit, when there is an instant negative consequence for doing it.

We'd both been Toastmaster International members in the past. (toastmasters.org learning how to speak in public) They have mastered this! There is a consequence for every mistake so you learn fast. She said the first time she was clapped down for going over time in her speech had such an impact; she was never not punctual again. I can relate.

In Toastmasters, while you are doing your presentation, someone is counting how many times you say "um and ah" and you pay for each one you say. I remember paying over a $1.00 for all my "ums" after only a 5-minute presentation. It bothered me that I had said that many "ums." It bothered me more that I had to pay for them! We had a very frugal upbringing. Dad was born in Scotland; he was an engineer, we weren't broke, yet we weren't allowed to have orange juice in the house as it was considered a luxury. We go to the football game saying "Get that quarterback!" So yeah, it bugged me paying for each "um."

So Wendy decides her team needs to have an instant consequence when they say "but" so they will quickly become aware and learn to change. They decide that day, anytime you hear someone say the word "but" you have to flick them on the upper arm with your finger. A few of them were complaining they were going to have deep bruises on their arms by the end of the day! Alas, a hard habit to break.

Swap out the words "but" "however" and "except" and replace them with either a "period" "pause" "and" or "yet"

Trigger #3: YOU

Again, during conflict, the higher the stress, the less likely we are tapped into our intelligence. Using the word "you" may trigger defensiveness and thus increase the stress.

"You are late." I'm being blamed!

If you instead use the word "I", you take away the potential trigger of blame and accusation. It now puts the onus, blame, or responsibility on you when you start with the word "I."

"I notice you are late."

Remember, how we perceive something determines how we feel about it. How we feel about it determines how we act on it. Many of these triggers are subconscious and we may not recognize their effects.

So, let's try this in a scenario using "I" instead of the word "you."

Your colleague is delegating a job to you. He wants to ensure there is no misunderstanding so he says, "Will you please repeat back what I said? I just want to make sure you got it right."

Now I like the first bit. It's very polite, "Will you please repeat back what I said." It's the second bit some of us might find rude;

"I just want to make sure you got it right."

When I ask in numerous events how many people find it rude, we tend to get 50% – 80% of the audience saying yes, it can seem rude when they say "I just want to make sure you got it right."

Different people react differently under stress. Depending on your personality style, I know some people with the personality style who will repeat it back wrong with intent just to piss them off for being rude to them in the first place. Burn!

Hear the difference using "I" instead of "you."

"Will you please repeat back what I said? I just
   want to ensure I was clear."

Wow, that's class! They are taking responsibility
for being clear - not potentially blaming you for not
getting it right in the first place. Your self-esteem is
still intact. They have created a safe environment for
communication. A potential trigger of conflict has
been avoided.

Swap out the word "You" and replace it with the word "I"

We all have triggers. Even the word "relax" may cause
a trigger. We know what the word relax means. Yet
many of us may have a guilt association to the word
"relax." Relax may trigger accusations of being lazy,
can't be bothered, non-productive. Telling someone
to relax may actually trigger being insulted. We've all
had formative years. We may not even know which
words trigger us or why. If I say I'm going to relax
tonight, I know I may have a guilt association to the
word relax. By saying, "I'm going to embrace the
sloth." It now comes across guilt free, more noble and
productive somehow.

It's good to be aware of what your triggers are.

Again, some of these triggers are so insidious we
don't really recognize how they affect us. In English
Canada, we don't really use the word "Ma'am" very

often. Yet it seems really common in the States to use the word Ma'am.

I was in my 30's when I started to spend more time in the States. At first when I was addressed as Ma'am, it sounded odd. It sounded like I was old. Wait a minute, are they insulting me? How dare they call me Ma'am! Call me chick, don't you dare call me Ma'am!

Now if you were French calling me Madam, no problem. That sounds sexy. I've learned to ignore that trigger when in America. I don't feel as tweaked when I'm called Ma'am. I have learned that it is in fact a common term and when I hear it, I just repeat it back in my head with a French accent. Then I feel good.

So funny, a woman at a seminar mentioned she had raised her children to be respectful and to use "Sir" when addressing an older man or one of authority to show respect. The school where her son went to called her in to discuss her son's disrespect of his teacher. The teacher had actually perceived the lad's use of the word "Sir" to be disrespectful and condescending. Amazing, isn't it?

Check out bonus tips at:

www.BeforeItHitsTheFan.com

Vocal

Your Tone Sets the Tone

Your tone of voice impacts the tone of the communication. It's possible we don't realize we've been under an accumulation of stress, how it affects our own voices, and how that tone affects others. Ever had a bad day at work, stressful traffic on the way home, and after such an accumulation of stress all day your voice is tense and terse? Ever tried that kind of voice on your teenager? Does it ever work? Don't they just tune you out and instead hear "wa-wa-wa-wa."

Some of us don't realize as our stress goes up, so does our pitch and speed of talk. The higher the pitch, the stronger it cuts through the air and becomes more irritatingly audible. Try this, whisper in a high-pitched voice then whisper in a low tone of voice. With a low tone it's far less audible. Consider it a bit more calming when one's voice is at a conversational tone and speed instead of a high pitched fast one.

Talking too fast in a high-pitched voice creates a feeling of communicating with a Chihuahua on steroids.

Take a deep breath.

Be aware that we tend to breathe shallow when stressed. Take a couple of deep breaths of air to oxygenate the system and calibrate your awareness of your tone. Watch the speed.

Here's a classic reaction. When the other person is stressed and uses a harsh tone of voice, sometimes we get triggered into matching that tone. We've heard misery loves company. When people are angry and upset, they want to drag you into their drama. It's like fishing. They want to pull you in. Don't bite the bait! Try this.

The louder they talk, the softer you respond.

Don't get sucked into other people's drama tones. We feel physically stressed when listening to a stressed out voice. Be aware not to fall into this dance. Don't match the stress, angst, or anger in their voice out of habit or out of a subconscious reaction. Try to find control in at least your pace and tone of voice.

You are Judged by Your Tone.

We may not even hear what the other person said. We've instead personally judged them on the tone of voice they used. Our emotions and stress levels affect the quality of our tone and the tone speaks louder than the content of our message.

If someone is really angry when they confront you with their conflict, and their tone of voice is loud and based in anger and aggression when they say,

"YOU ARE LATE." What do you hear? "Boy, they are out of control" That's what you hear.

If their voice is really emotional, upset, shaky, "You (gasp for air a few times) are late (as the voice carries up in pitch)" What do you hear? "Boy, are they ever emotional."

If it's one of those irritating, condescending, blaming, nagging, down and trodden depressive voices like Eeyore the Donkey character from *Winnie the Pooh* dragging out every syllable in a whining voice,

"I caaaan't belieeeeeve you are laaaaaaaate" What do you interpret that to be? "Kill me now!"

It's the emotion in the voice that stands out in the message. Their character is judged by it and reflected in it. That's what they hear over the content of the message.

Of course it's normal for our emotions to come out in our tone of voice. I'm not saying to never do this. I'm saying for the purpose of "mastering the moment in conflict resolution" when brought into a conflict, be hyper aware of your tone and speed of voice during conflict.

Here's one of my favourite tips. Whether it's you, them, or both of you stressed. To ensure they hear what you said without triggering more conflict by a tone in your voice. Just say whatever you need to say in the same tone of voice as if you are at the dinner table saying,

"Pass the bread, please."

It's calm, cool, collected. Careful though. It needs to sound neutral, not condescending. If it sounds condescending, that tends to makes the conflict worse. Make it as neutral, natural and conversational as saying,

"The movie starts at 7:15"

"I may need directions to the train station"

"Put the syrup on the table beside the waffles"

"Pass the bread, please"

I've had so much fun with the "pass the bread" voice! In training events this is one of the big takeaways for most people! Just being 'aware' of how our tone of voice comes across and how our tone is so easily hijacked by our moods and emotions is huge. To be aware of it and gain a sense of control in controlling our tone during conflict has an instant effect.

See how easy and kind of fun it is to say these next few phrases in a neutral tone. Go on, give it a try! Say it out loud as you read these examples in your "pass the bread" tone,

> "I noticed you were 15 minutes late yesterday"

> "Productivity has gone down 45% since you hired Z last year"

> "I'd like you to take the 7:15 flight"

See how easy that was? Let's try a few more . . .

> "Why yes that was my husband's lap you spent the evening sitting on last night."

> "I couldn't help but overhear you tell Jackie I was a stupid cow and it sounded like an insult, did I misunderstand anything?"

> "You can have my respect, you don't need to raise your voice to get it."

> "Pass the bread, please."

Obviously I'm having a bit of fun with this to make a point. You are judged by your tone.

When you find yourself in a conflict conversation, be aware of your tone of voice. Keep your pace and your pitch calm and conversational. Take a deep breath of air and remind yourself to say whatever you need to say in the same tone of voice as if you were at the dinner table saying, "Pass the bread, please."

In Most Cases, the Truth is in the Tone.

This is a wee bit more challenging to cover in print form instead of in audio form. If you say to someone "Boy, YOU really look intelligent today" in a tone that oozes sarcasm and loathing, clearly anyone listening is going to know what you really mean is the complete opposite.

If someone yells in a an angered voice, "I'M FINE" clearly we've understood they are anything but fine. We'll probably also judge them as being out of control. We will feel and/or react to the effects of the high conflict environment they are creating. Instead of hearing they are fine, we're thinking, "Look out, run away, this person isn't fine, this person is nuts!"

Our emotional state is reflected in our tone of voice. This is normal and natural. When pressure, emotions, and conflict goes up, without even trying, the emotional state we are feeling seems to automatically make it's presence in our tone of voice. This can be a good thing when you are listening to the other person during conflict.

During a conflict, we may not be thinking as clearly. In the moment of conflict, we are temporarily compromised from our reasoning abilities. The driving emotion may be a gut instinct or reaction. The words we chose while we are going through these emotions may not always be well thought out.

Remember, a legal document becomes null and void if signed under stress or duress.

So if their tone is laced with a particular emotion, don't focus too much on what they are actually saying, instead focus on their tone of voice. See if you can't figure out the emotional force behind it. It's hard to solve the actual problem when the emotions are high. It's like the angry customer reaming you out on the phone. If you allow them to vent and get the stress out, they then can start to think more rationally. That's when they are able to apologize for their behaviour after they get rid of the emotional bubble. They are in a position to think more clearly.

So here's a consideration, if you can tell the person is really angry, don't ignore the anger. Instead of ignoring the anger, grab it and acknowledge it so you can get it out of the way. Once the high emotion is reduced, clarity of thought can start to happen.

If they sound really angry, in your polite "pass the bread" voice, what if you were to say, "I can understand how angry you must feel as a result of this situation." Aaaaaa, they feel heard. Some of the emotional pressure can now seep out. It's not bottled up.

If they sound really frustrated, "I can appreciate how frustrating this situation must be for you." Aaaaa, they feel heard. More stress is let out, more logic and calm thought can come in.

"Listen with the intent to understand, not the intent to reply"
-Stephen Covey

Out of our best intentions, we may ignore their emotion in the hopes of keeping it from getting worse. Sometimes ignoring it makes it worse. As humans, we want to feel heard. It feels rude being ignored and that in and of itself will create more conflict. It's OK to acknowledge something bad. It can be therapeutic. "You gotta grieve it to leave it." It helps to be able to bring up the problem and how it makes you feel so you can take a look at it, acknowledge it, and let it go.

Visual

Fun Facts:

Your eyes are an extension of your brain.

- Of all of the sensory organs in the human body, your eyesight is the only sensory organ that has brain cells in it!
- It only takes 1/10th of a second to pick up a visual read or a sense of a visual. That's about the same amount of time as it takes to blink your eyes!
- 4/5ths of all the impressions on the senses come from the eye.
- Visuals in our brains are processed 60,000 times faster than text.

That's really interesting! But wait, there's more. . .

Ever heard of micro expressions? Dr Paul Ekman, who is famous for his work in studying facial expression and emotion, came up with the term. He was also named one of the 100 most influential people in the world by TIME Magazine.

Micro expressions are facial expressions that occur within $1/25^{th}$ of a second. They are involuntary and expose a person's true emotions.These facial expressions are universal. The TV show "Lie to Me" was loosely based on Dr. Ekman. The show was about being able to read body language and micro expressions; stress, psychological discomfort, anxiety, dislike, issues, or tension.

Everyone flashes micro expressions and no one can hide them. Who knew!

So does that mean that basically every human being on the planet has the same facial expression for the same emotions, unless they are a sociopath?

Body language works subconsciously

If the visual has such a huge impact, then why am I bumping into trainers who are still teaching that the impact on the words, tone, and body language in the Total Communication Package is: 7% words, 38% tone, 55% body language! Doesn't this information on our eyes and the visual blow that peasley 55% out of the water! Is it possible we focus a disproportionate amount of time on just our words when learning how to become better communicators? There are a lot of great resources out there to learn more about body language and micro expressions. Any small tip or new information can change how you see your whole world and how you act within it as a result.

Ever heard the term Active Listening? Is that term clearly defined? Would everyone you ask have the same description of what active listening means? Voila, another example of general, ambiguous, language that is open to interpretation. Does it mean you should be doing jumping jacks while listening to show you are active?

Some examples of active listening would be to listen to the words they say. Listen to the tone. The truth is in the tone and the tone may give insight to their emotional state. Another example of active listening is to,

Listen with your eyes. Watch their body language.

Do you ever stop to think about what your body language or facial expression is saying to others? Back in my late 20's I was working as a flight attendant for Air Canada. An exciting time when they had just become officially bilingual and I had just moved back to Canada after recently learning French. During a long international flight, the head flight attendant came up to me and said, "You are positive, really professional, great to work with, but you've got the most amazing deadpan fish face I've ever seen." My mouth dropped open so wide hearing this I probably looked like a dying Bass! I mean who really looks at their facial expressions all day long? I tried to force some kind of a smile on my face. Instead, it looked like someone you'd want to avoid as it didn't look natural. It took a while to learn how to have a pleasant resting face.

I hear so many participants say how frustrating it is when their colleagues assume a wrong impression based on their facial expression. It is quite common. One manager had a disgruntled employee in his office complaining. The manager's intent, focus and desire was to listen to what the employee was saying. Even though everything the manager did, what he said, and how he said it was respectful, the employee came to the conclusion her boss didn't care and didn't like her solely because his face had a resting, non-expressive look.

Look, there are lots of reasons why our body language may be misinterpreted. A manager who came to chat with me during a break at a workshop was so worried about crossing her arms. She did it all the time and feared she may be giving a wrong message or causing conflict by doing so. She didn't want her subordinates to think she was disinterested, disagreeing, or disengaging and fretted about how to stop this habit she has. It's really common to cross one's arms and it doesn't have to be a bad thing.

Women especially. We may cross our arms because we are cold. Women may be going through hot and cold flashes and feel temperature changes more. Is it a hot flash, or a power surge? It's just comfortable to have one's arms crossed without meaning anything by it.

Those who are more introverted may cross their arms to give a sense of comfortable distance. It can be a subtle way of letting someone know you are not open to a hug. Some women who have large breasts may subconsciously have their arms crossed over their chests to hide their size. I can't relate to that. I got my cleavage on the wrong end. So I could instead cross my arms and lift up to create the impression there is cleavage.

Here are some tips on body language during conflict:

Be on the same level and at a respectful distance

If the angry person is standing above you looking down on you, stand up to create an equal and respectful environment. Give them ample space of respect. Or turn a bit to your side to deflect some of the anger. You don't have to say a word. By standing up at a respectful distance, subconsciously you are letting them know you don't want to be talked down to. The playing field is fair, equal. Ensure you give ample distance between you and them. Doing this could have completely adverse effects in some cultures so remember, it depends.

Give a little more space and protect yours

It's an aggressive move to get into someone's personal physical space and comfort zone. Be cognizant of reducing conflict by staying away from theirs, obviously. Maybe something new to do would be to purposely move further back just a bit more. As long as it seems normal to do so. Try using any of these tips so you can be aware in the moment during conflict.

If they get into your space, be aware of the trigger you may instinctively feel. Don't let yourself react to it without thought. Move so you have your personal space. Your intent is to reduce conflict, not trigger it in others, nor be triggered yourself.

Be at an angle, not right in front of them - especially men

When sitting or standing, place yourself to their side so your head is turned a bit when looking at them instead of face to face or directly in front of them. It creates a more conversational environment. It is less confrontational than being in front of them. Even a small turn of the body or small step to the side can change the dynamics.

This is more of an important issue when it comes to men. When men are stressed, they pump way more testosterone into their system. If there is some conflict and stress between two men, by action of standing in front of the other may trigger alpha dog; more competitive, more aggressive, more fight, more win, solve, fix. Could be a flick of the finger instinct. If you stand a bit to the side so your torsos are not directly in front of the other can reduce it. If it's a man and a women, or two women, it doesn't have the same testosterone trigger, just man and man be aware of this body positioning.

Tilt your head a bit when they are speaking

Ever so subtle When you see someone's head tilted to the side while they are listening to you, it gives the impression they are really listening. That's because we do that when we are riveted to someone's every word, pondering their message, letting our brain do its work by tilting the head. So try just tilting your head. Obviously you need to listen. Yet this way may trigger a positive perception of you and reduce their stress and defensiveness.

Use a vulnerable position to defuse an aggressive one

Remember, it only takes 1/10th of a second to visually register this in the brain. To reduce conflict or potential conflict, by displaying a vulnerable body positioning shows you are not a threat.

Animals do this all the time. A dog wants to let other people or other dogs know that it is friendly.

The dog wants to decrease the element of conflict. It doesn't want you to attack. It shows a vulnerable position, giving you permission to come closer and giving up the alpha to the other. You've seen this; a dog will lie down on it's back displaying its underside. No bones of protection there!

The dog is panting away, wagging its tail, giving out this vibe, "Look how friendly I am. You could eviscerate me but I'm sure you won't because I am so friendly!"

So to translate that into human body language examples as I can't help but imagine someone going into the horizontal position on the ground panting with their arms out. Tilting your head to the side is an example. By doing so, you are displaying your jugular. Doesn't take long to bleed out if that gets slit. Having your hands out so the underside of your wrists are displayed when arms are down has an open feel to it. Show a little palm.

If you really want to cross your arms . . .

Do so in the way that the topside of your fingers are showing on both hands. The hands are not hidden. Or if it doesn't look unnatural for you to do so, cup your hands and hold your elbows. Both hands are more visible, albeit not the inside palm area. Both are out in the open and it has a slightly hugging, nurturing, supporting aura about it.

If you think you are going to cry . . .

Look up and blink. Breathe. Take a slow deep full breath right now. Feel that. Remember, we tend to breath shallow when stressed. The key is to look up and blink.

So this is a time you may want to sit down so the other person is above you. Easier to segue this move into your repertoire as it looks less strange for you to be looking up when you are sitting down. Or position yourself in a way that it seems more natural to look in an upwardly direction. Pretend you are pondering some mathematical question. I'll explain more about this in the next bit.

The Next Bit . . .

It's not just how people perceive your body language.

You can change how you think, feel, and act by changing your body positioning.

Your eyes

Take the example of the eyes and where to look to avoid crying. When you look up, you are connected to thinking person mode. We often intuitively look up when retrieving a memory or, when creatively thinking about how to make something up. When we look down, we are more connected to our emotions. When sad, devastated, grieving, forlorn, depressed, in full sobbing mode, we are usually looking down and with our head down.

So the next time you feel your eyes burning and you think you may cry, asap LOOK UP, blink, breath. Don't look down! Once you look down, and the floodgates open, you're screwed. There is no stopping them. Look up, blink, breath. There are many more tips on what to do to not cry yet this one is a big one and is very effective. Can even try it at a tear jerker movie to see how it works.

I reconnected with a woman after she had been at an event with me where I was talking about women in business, handling conflict, and managing emotions. She came up to tell me how she had tried the tips on how not to cry and was so pleased and surprised with how well it worked! You see her dog had died. Clearly anyone would be upset. She still had to go to work and function. So any time thoughts of her dog and sadness of loss seeped into her thoughts, she'd look up, blink and breath. The moment passed, she avoided the tears, avoided having others at work see her tears, and was able to continue on with work. It's not easy to schedule in what time you are going to grieve. Sometimes we don't want others to see us cry.

Posture

When in a conflictual conversation with someone, if we curl in, we may succumb more to the feelings of weakness and disempowerment in the moment. Sure we look more vulnerable (as we covered when that can be appropriate in a previous section) yet the point in this section is about how to change how you feel. We intuitively curl in when mourning or feeling sad and defeated. To tap into feeling a sense of strength, confidence, and empowerment, pretend there is a string in your solar plexus pulling you up to the heavens above. Feel your posture tall and straight. Try it. Curl yourself in, then stand straight and tall. Instantly you can feel a difference.

Breathe deeply and let it fill your chest

Deep full breaths of air helps you feel a sense of calm. Controlling the breath gives you something to focus on when the challenging person is talking to you. Fill your lungs with an invisible energy and sense of calm and fullness in your heart and chest area. Be aware of not breathing shallow.

Change how you feel with a smile

Try putting a smile on your face. A big manic smile. Head up, show those teeth. Try it now. You feel better and happier, don't you? It's hard to feel mad or sad when you have a huge smile on your face. Now don't get me wrong. I'm not suggesting that when someone starts a communication of conflict with you that you put a big huge smile on your face.

Mind you, it might reduce the conflict immediately because the other person may fear you've gone a bit batty looking like that.

Yet what if you are on the phone with someone and you feel your confidence and happy disposition is being sucked out of you as a result of how you feel as they are communicating to you. Stand up tall, fill your lungs with the energy of oxygen, put a big smile on your face. They can't see you. As a bonus, if you catch a reflection or glimpse of yourself doing this in a mirror, it almost makes you want to laugh. You'll look pretty funny doing it, thus cheering yourself up even more.

Woo-hoo! I won!!

You won the race! You won the lottery! Bingo! The team you are so invested in made an amazing and completely unexpected winning goal at the last second of the game! Wow, the exhilaration! You fling your arms up in the air in absolute victory, joy, happiness, celebration. Throwing your arms up in the air makes you feel fantastic! Exhilarated! Powerful! Again, it may not be appropriate to do this while the other person can see you. Try it when on the phone, while reading a mean email, or maybe you can step away from sight for a few seconds to do a few "Woo-Hoo" arm gestures.

If you know you will be dealing with conflict, try doing these physical tips in private before you are face to face with them.

I was working with the complaint department of a huge company on how to reduce stress and manage emotions. Their whole job all day long was dealing with complaining customers! They loved this tip and implemented it all day long! Before work, at the very end of their break before getting back to work, between phone calls or bathroom breaks they would stand tall with their arms high in the hair. Just for a few moments. Either hold your arms up in a big V between your head, or pump your arms up and down above your shoulders.

There is a great TED talk by Amy Cuddy about this I'd highly recommend you watch. She'll go far more in depth and you'll benefit from her expertise in this area.

How you feel determines how you act. If you can change your body positioning to trigger feelings of happiness during or before a conflict, you'll be less likely to take things personally, feel defensive, or angry. You will listen differently. When you are happy, you are tapped into your intelligence and can think better.

You Can't Make Informed Decisions Without the Information

- Lorna McLaren

The Importance of Facts and Specifics

Facts:

If you stay with facts, you will be safe. You can't negate facts. Feelings are not wrong yet feelings are not always clearly defined and we may feel differently at different times. Feelings are open to interpretation. When it comes to communicating with diplomacy, you will find common ground and safety if you stay with facts. **Fact: You are reading this.** How you *feel* about reading it is a different matter.

Specifics:

If we say things in a general, ambiguous, airy-fairy way, we lose control on how it will be interpreted. Misunderstandings create the perfect breeding ground for future conflict. Being specific increases your credibility, reduces misunderstandings, and has more impact.

Imagine you are screening through resumes looking for a receptionist. One resume says, "Answered phones" I'm sure you're not thinking, "Who knew?" It's a fact, yet it doesn't have much impact. The other one gives a specific example. "Handled a three line telephone system with 46 employees." Who are you going to call for the interview?

In conflict resolution, we need to ask for clarification, specifics, or examples so we have the information we need to make informed decisions.

As an example, let's say a colleague comes up to you at work and says, "Sometimes I feel like you don't treat me with respect." That is good information to know! Yet is it specific? Is it clearly defined? No! It is general and open to interpretation.

I'm not saying they are wrong in how they feel. They have every right to feel a certain way. I'm just questioning the fact that it is not specific which leaves you at an impasse. You don't have enough information to make an informed decision. It's like those never-ending projects at work. Nine times out of ten, a project becomes never-ending because it wasn't clearly defined in the first place.

What if you were to say, "Thank you for letting me know. Would you please give me a specific example so I may better understand what you mean? Wow, that's class! Let's break it down:

1. "Thank you for letting me know." It's polite. It shows appreciation and respect. That phrase

creates a safe environment for communication to continue.

2. "Can you please give me . . ." There is something very polite and disarming about 'Can you please'. You are not telling them what to do, nor making demands. You've shown a direct interest in hearing more from them. Getting their perspective.

3. ". . . a specific example . . . " It brings it back to finding out the Fact of what actually happened to create their feeling of being disrespected. Can't negate facts.

4. ". . . so I may better understand what you mean." You are speaking to them, showing you care about them, and want to understand them.

Let's say they respond with, "Well here's an example. You took my parking spot every day last week and you slashed my tires this morning." That's more more specific, isn't it? Now you know what is going on and what specifically caused the feeling of disrespect.

If I were to say to you, "You're always late, you're never on time" Well first off, who's motivated by blame and accusation? That wording alone will spark conflict. Secondly, I come across as some airy-fairy flake. Clearly I don't have a clue what I'm talking about. I'm using blame and accusation. When in life is something a never or an always? Yet what if I actually knew the facts. What if I actually knew how late you were? So instead of saying, "You're always late and never on time." I could say "I notice you've been 15 minutes late every Thursday for seven years now." It's a fact. Can't negate facts.

Personal attack: "He's too lazy to answer the phone."

Fact: "He lost 17 calls to voicemail."

When you know what's going on, you have the facts, you'll exude a natural confidence when you communicate. I'll bet if someone asked you the name of your children, or the name of your parents, or siblings, or good friends, you'd exude a natural confidence when answering. You're not bragging. You know this information to be factual truth without a doubt.

Sometimes the biggest fear is fear of the unknown. Anytime we don't feel a sense of control, stress goes up. It's like being hired for a job and they don't give you a job description. How do you know when you're done? Even if it's horrific what you are going through. Let's say your loved one is in the hospital. You don't know if they are going to live or die. So stressful not knowing. Yet once you have found out what is happening with that person, you have the facts, be it good or bad, then you can come to terms with it.

You can't make informed decisions without the information

With conflict, try to get the information you need so you may feel a sense of control, confidence and support. Gaining intel is an intelligent move and intuitively adds confidence. Every master negotiator will tell you - the person with the most information has more control in how the negotiation goes. Every master negotiator will tell you to let them go first. Get their information first. Ignorance is not bliss. Ignorance is a recipe for disaster.

Be aware that some people, with intent, will not give you the information you need. That way, you won't have a sense of control. Anytime we don't have a sense of control stress goes up.

Way back in the day, in the school marking system, they used something called a bell curve. There is no control in a bell curve! Every student could be an "A" student, but the teacher is only allowed to give out two "A's" on the bell curve! When I taught in a college, if a student wanted to get a good mark, they knew in advance the assignments they had to do. They knew in advance to what specifications to get the good mark. A sense of control reduces stress. Get the information you need before you can make an informed decision.

People Rarely Argue With Their Own Information

- Lorna McLaren

This is a wonderful tip to use especially when perceptions on both sides could be quite different. It can also be a safe choice to use this particular tip if the person you are having a conflict with is in a higher level of authority than you are.

It is also a nice accompaniment when dealing with one who is struggling with low self-esteem. Examples of that could be a "know it all" who is not inclined to listen to anyone else in the first place. The big ego person as the ego display may be a front when someone doesn't feel confident about themselves in the first place. Some people try to force respect with a show instead of earn respect with their actions. Works beautifully with someone who tends to externalize everything. You know the type who blames everyone else instead of being responsible for themselves? They are never accountable, oh no siree. Or for those who don't feel heard, valued, or appreciated.

Also, there are certain personality styles who are motivated by defiance. They are almost wired to do the opposite of what you ask. Ring any bells when you think of the puberty and teenage years? Being defiant seems to be a right of passage during that stage in life. It is a time of inward focus and learning to be independent. A break from the control of one's parents or authority is a part of growing up.

Using this tip can:

- reduce stress for both of you
- provide you with the information you need to make an informed decision
- take the stress off of you having to come up with the right thing to say in an unexpected conflict
- give you some time to think before you respond
- allow the other person to feel heard and being "heard" in and of itself reduces stress.

So instead of the stress of thinking you have to be the one to "solve it" or tell them what to do, simply let them talk. They will agree with their own information as they are the ones saying it!

During conflict, that other person may be a wee bit more defensive if and when someone tells them what to do or how to think. They may not be as open to listen to you. They are focused on themselves. So let the focus be their own information. Already some stress and conflict will be reduced. Who needs the extra stress of trying to get your point in when they won't listen anyway, right? Time and place.

Here is another situation where you see this happen:

Let's say for example you work with Chris and Frieda and you've become friends. Chris invites you to a big dinner party Saturday night where they are going to be giving an award to Frieda; she's done a great job. Well you like Chris and you like Frieda but you don't want to go to some boring social event on the weekend for people at work! You're busy, you want to hang with your family or relax, not do something work related. Yet you fear if you are honest and say, "I don't want to go" you may cause some conflict or bad feelings with your peers. So you decide to make up an excuse to get out of it.

> "Thanks for the invite, Chris. I'd love to go. I know how much Frieda deserves the award but shoot; I've got a date that night. I guess I can't go. What a shame, I really wish I could."

Well what if Chris says, "No problem, bring your date. We'd love to have them! I know your mom's in town, bring your mom and bring the kids too. Free shrimp! See you at 7:00, OK?"

Now what have you got to do?

You basically have one of two choices:

1) Find a date and show up
2) Make up another lie to get out of it

Why? When it comes to the human factor, we don't want to feel humiliated. We don't want to lose face. We don't want to get caught in a lie.

Like the phrases, "Your word is your law, your word is your bond." "When you say it, you own it." So get their information first . . . then use it against them. (insert evil wicked laugh mwahahahahaha)

I'm kind of kidding. And then again, I'm kind of not kidding. Think about it, if you stay with the information they provide, you'll have less conflict as you are using the information they supplied in the first place.

I use this tip with my mother all the time.

Allow me to set the stage. My mother is very proud and stubborn. She does not like being told what to do and is an independent thinker. Nothing wrong with that per se. Her own mother had been very controlling and not very nice. Adopted at the age of two with her twin sister. The father was a business owner, jolly disposition. The mother was evil. The mother controlled what the twins wore, when they were allowed to smile, and often disciplined with the reminder that if they didn't do what they were told, they'd be sent to an orphanage. She ate with silver cutlery, lived in a large house, the best education, white gloves at tea parties. Yet she was not allowed to feel proud of her accomplishments or capabilities. Even when she was on the honour roll at school, her mother would say, "Well, I guess you got the brains but, clearly your sister got the looks." They're almost identical!! So rightly so, my mother has a thing about being told what to do and triggered if accused of not being intelligent. She studied science in University and has a degree. She went off to India to study yoga as part of her transition once the children were raised. She is a cool lady.

At the time of this story, my mother is in her early-80's and had been living alone for over 35 years on a small island a short ferry ride from Vancouver. She has led a physically fit and healthy lifestyle, ex-yoga teacher, eats wholesome food, loves to laugh and commune with nature. Great shape for her age! She was having some symptoms, I took her to see her Doctor. A big part was not being hydrated. Four cups of coffee a day and a small glass of organic orange juice at breakfast was it. I had recently moved back to Vancouver and hadn't thought about or noticed her liquid consumption habits when I visit her. I mean, who does?

She follows Dr.'s advice except for the drinking liquids part. Next visit, Dr. says she needs to drink more fluids. No matter how often we discuss it, put glasses of water out in strategic areas (some with lemon wedges to entice), encourage, logically discuss drinking more fluids, it becomes a big conflict on her end. She becomes defensive and defiant. Her response is how healthy she is, takes no medication, leads a healthy lifestyle, she knows best, don't tell her what to do, scientific mind.

And the drama of family continues . . .

Even gently and politely pleading with her to have just a couple of small glasses more of any fluid a day became a conflict, then accusation, and stress. Why there is conflict over drinking more water for one's health and wellbeing is mind boggling! She is a stubborn woman.

People Rarely Argue With Their Own Information

Key bits of Information:

- To be treated with respect
- She is in good health
- Not being controlled
- Capable of making her own decisions
- Educated with a scientific mind

So next Dr. visit, I had him write a prescription to drink four glasses of water a day and put it on her fridge. The higher authority of a prescription seemed to work for about a week. Then the conflict returned.

Next visit to her home is for a few days. I tried showing her articles in newspapers and on my laptop of the importance of drinking water from medical and scientific standpoints. By not doing so, how detrimental it can be on one's health. I reinforced her information from an educated point of view. "You have a scientific mind, I thought you would find this interesting" as I pass her an article with proof, facts and photos on the importance of drinking enough water and why.

Of course I am communicating to her with extra respect and appreciation. She deserves it. This is an example of stubbornness to the extreme and how it triggers conflict.

I see her registering this information and actually showing signs of being open to agree with it. Good so far. She drank her four glasses that day without mention. The next day, I could see her losing interest. Hmmm, so I tried her other bits of key information; health, she has to be in control to make the decision for herself, and she is capable of making good decisions.

It is important to use facts (can't negate facts). The local newspaper had an article about a marathon coming up with athletes from around the world. They were asking for volunteers to help at the water stations among other things. It was like a surreal coincidence! What an opportunity. Over lunch we discussed the article. I didn't mention a thing about the water. Focused only on healthy people, disciplined in a really healthy diet and exercise. Like she was. A value she upholds.

Over coffee, I brought up some stories from being a volunteer ski patroller. During athletic events, we would be there and available for first aid purposes. Always with oxygen bottles and water. I shared no matter how healthy and incredibly fit these people were, the moment they succumb to any dehydration or issues with altitude (so I didn't sound too obvious), they are out of the race.

I complimented her on her choice to take care of her health. No medications, better shape than most people of her age, and she had a happy attitude about her. She chose to be happy and do her best to be opposite from her mother and how that contributes to her health. It was a good decision. Told her I was proud of her. And it's true. One of my mother's most common topics is how difficult her mother was so it was easy to wait until it came up. She drank her water after that and continued to do so. Her decision based on her information. No argument. Conflict be gone.

It's Smart to Know When You're Stupid

- Lorna McLaren

Stress and the Human Factor

Every one of us is difficult when stressed. When emotions, pressure, stress, and conflict, goes up, where does our logic go? As stress goes up, our brain starts to disengage from the frontal lobes of reasoning. It reengages to that primal, reptilian, knee jerk part of the brain triggering an acute stress response. The fight or flight response. Blood is leaving the organs to send oxygenated blood to the muscles. It causes the release of a hormone called cortisol.

At that particular time we're not as wired or tapped into our rational abilities. During stress, recognize we may be temporarily compromised from our ability to think as clearly or as reasonably. It's smart for us to know that. Just being aware can give us more of a sense of control.

Do you know anyone who works in a law firm? Here's a fact. A legal document becomes null and void if signed under stress or duress.

We all have 20/20 vision hindsight. Yet in the heat of the moment when stress is high, it's hard to tap into our intelligence.

Here is an extreme example

Let's say you're being publicly humiliated in front of your family, friends, and peers. Someone is cutting you down, ostracizing and berating you. You're shocked, you're humiliated, you don't have a clue what to say, you're speechless! All you can do is stand there and speak Guppy! (that's when your mouth silently drops open and shut with each insult thrown your way). And then you think of the perfect comeback . . . at 2 o'clock in the morning. "I should have said that!" Didn't Seinfeld do a whole show on what George wished he had said! The brain comes up with the answers you ask of it, sometimes you don't know when.

We all have epiphanies, revelations, and resolutions that just pop into our heads. We rarely get these epiphanies when we are running back and forth between meetings, projects, multi-tasking and under pressure. Isn't it usually during times of rest and relaxation that those epiphanies come? In the middle of the night, waking up, in the shower, skiing the trees, fly fishing, being in nature, relaxing and reflecting.

Ever been in a bad mood while writing that scathing email and then press send? Ahhh! Yet if you wait 24 hours before sending it, you can re-read it when you are thinking more clearly. All of us are difficult when stressed.

You may have heard of the H.A.L.T. acronym.

These are times when you will most likely be more stressed and possibly less capable of handling conflict as rationally.

H
is for Hungry

I don't know about you, but when I'm ravenous, I'm a ratbag! It's quite common to feel angrier when one is hungry. Many of us notice this more as we get older. When your blood sugar is getting low.

Your brain takes up about 2% of your body mass. It absorbs over 20% of your calorie needs. The brain uses more energy than any other human organ!

There is a lot of fat in the brain. Foods high in antioxidants keep the free radicals from getting to the brain. Your brain is an energy hound! The types of food you eat can have a direct impact on how you feel. Glucose powers up the brain. One prune has huge amounts of antioxidants and is really good for the brain. Also good for the process of elimination . . .

At a minimum, don't do your conflict resolution before lunch

Do it after lunch. Do it when you have some energy in your veins and brain. You'll probably think better and be in a better mood. It's like the cardinal rule for training events or long meetings,

Feed them and they will come.

Having nutritional food available will boost your ability to think more efficiently. Better yet, ensure you have your own good eating habits and have food available when you need a rescue. Chocolate didn't make the top 20 foods for the brain yet it's pretty close up there in being high in antioxidants. The darker the better it is for the brain. If you are serious about your health, get the good quality chocolate.

My fellow business travelers know how hard it can be to eat properly when dashing to a flight right after work to get to the next city! So many delays and being hijacked by limited choices of heavy overpriced food is an added insult. Sometimes you are foiled at security. I've had a mini single serving tin of tuna as my only backup snack for a foodless flight stop me with TSA. Fish is good for the brain and it was removed from my possession accused of being a liquid! No matter how I promised I wasn't going to drink it, they wouldn't let me bring it on my bunny hop flights.

For those of us with a substance abuse problem with chocolate, having those chocolate flavour protein (healthy, not laced with sugar) meal replacement drinks or bars can help tremendously in holding you over between meals. There is something comforting about chocolate. Almonds and certain nuts are good for the brain and easy to carry, too.

A
is for the Accumulation of Stress; angry, agitated, anxious

Sometimes we don't realize we've been through a bunch of little stressors already and we must realize how all those little stressors add up. Ever had a bad day at work, everything goes wrong, and then you take it out on traffic? It's like the George Carlin joke: Everyone you pass is an idiot. Everyone who passes you is a maniac. Or you take your stress out on you and/or your family when you get home? Tense voice, tense body, short of patience, irritable.

Maybe you are an Occupational Extrovert. Perhaps you are more introverted by nature yet you have to be 'on' and extroverted because of your job requirements. By the end of the day, you're done. All you want to do is be alone. It's just too much being around people all day long. Instead of recognizing you need to recharge your batteries throughout the day in reducing or slowing the pent up frustration, you instead take it out on your family. "Spouse, leave me alone. Kids, go play hide and seek" and then you don't even bother looking for them for at least 30 minutes while you try to get some alone time.

Be very aware if you are already compromised with the accumulation of past stressors. Stress manifests physically. It's in our language. Where do you hold the weight of responsibility? On your shoulders. She's a pain in the butt. He's a pain in the neck. They make me sick.

You can't control all stress. You can control stress reduction

There are many things you can do with intent to reduce stress. Be proactive. Consider it vital to your health and wellbeing to continuously be aware of and act on reducing stress throughout the day. Heading into conflict when already stressed is best avoided. It is not a fair playing field if you are mentally compromised so don't be the one to throw yourself into the ring.

"Effective communication is a thinking person's sport"

- L. McLaren

Think preventative measures. If you feel an accumulation of stress weighing on you all day long, you'll be more primed to be in reactive mode if conflict unexpectedly knocks on your door. If you schedule in certain times throughout the day to reduce stress, you will be able to think more clearly when the unexpected conflict lands on your lap. Emotions and stress won't be so close to the surface. That just makes sense. Remember, stress when buried alive will manifest physically and mentally. Like letting some air out of the tire so it doesn't explode when it hits a bump. It can absorb it. Destressing is like having shock absorbers on.

Some people work out on a regular basis. They don't just wait until the end of the day to see if there is time. They schedule it in. They know if they don't schedule it in, it ain't happening. They know the exercise will reduce stress, help them think with calm focus, and feel better physically as well. Exercise helps keep the brain and the body from atrophying.

Stress is so insidious and we may not be aware how much of it we are taking on. It can come out in so many different ways.

Stress feeds on negative thoughts. Now imagine if you had a bad day when everything went wrong. You just got into your car about to enter rush hour traffic. But you knew you had a winning lottery ticket in your back pocket and you'd be 1 million dollars richer once you get to the store! If so, would any of those stressors from the day piss you off? Probably not. You'd be excitedly thinking about your unstoppable future.

Before all those little stressors accumulate and weigh you down, get a sense of control by intentionally reducing stress throughout the day.

L
is for Lonely

Anytime we feel alone in a situation, stress goes up. If we feel no one understands us, no one supports us, stress goes up.

We can feel alone when we don't know what's going on. Remember, you can't make informed decisions without the information. At a minimum, if you have the information you need, you have the facts; you will feel the support of the truth behind you. Maybe before you consider addressing a particular conflict, ensure you have enough information to support you, or ensure you have the support of others. When it comes to humans, we're not successful without the support of others. Just knowing someone supports us or believes in us is huge!

During a management-training event, Jill, a nurse who worked in palliative care, shared a situation that happened to her. Jill had had a really stressful week. She had worked long hours, had lost 2 patients who had succumbed to their illness, one of her children was struggling at school, and her husband had been laid off. I think nurses are amazing in what they do and during all of this, Jill seemed to be handling her job ok. And then a family member of a patient treated Jill in a very rude, condescending, angry and disrespectful way. Accused her of something that didn't happen. It was a misunderstanding.

That's when she lost it. As this person was taking it out on her, Jill politely excused herself and walked into her manager's office. She burst into tears. Everything just welled up from the nightmares of the week. She could hardly articulate a word as she vented to her manager. As Jill is recounting this story to me, her big concern was that she was going to get in trouble with her boss. As Jill had hit her breaking point, she feared how she came across, feared her boss would find her emotionally unstable or compromised from her ability to do her job. Her job meant so much to her, she was good at it. She was just so overwhelmed.

Her manager respectfully let Jill vent. After Jill was done, her manager reached over, put her hand gently on Jill's shoulder and simply said, "Jill, I support you." That gesture alone had instant impact! It meant so much to her to know her boss supported her, was there for her, believed in her, and understood how hard it can be. She felt less alone. It increased her feelings of goodwill towards her boss and her job.

New managers sometimes feel alone in their situation. It is hard to define the balance of boss, friend, colleague, subordinate. You may also feel alone if your HR department or your direct supervisor doesn't support you in how you would like to deal with a problem employee.

T
is for Tired

It's hard to think straight when tired. The brain continues to learn and percolate when we sleep. The less sleep we get, the stupider we become. Ever heard of college and university students pulling an all nighter cramming for the exam? They tend to get amnesia the next day.

One of the quickest routes to insanity is sleep deprivation. It's a proven form of torture. You may have noticed it during the newborn stages when you can't get enough sleep, or on a long flight with jet lag and time zone changes.

Stress will always compromise your ability to sleep; intermittent sleep, insomnia, or perhaps you sleep 6 hours yet your jaws are aching from grinding your teeth all night.

These days we are hearing more and more about the importance of having enough sleep. A lack of fitful sleep is bad for our brain, bad for our health, bad for our weight. A tired person driving shows the same habits as a drunk driver. Our sleep is precious and we must guard it!

Some have a guilt association around the word relax

In our society, have you ever noticed people almost bragging that they, "Worked a 10 hour day.

Only had 4 hours sleep. Didn't have time for a break." It is as if they are saying, "Oh look how productive, worthy and dedicated I am." Burned out workaholics are not good for business.

What an appropriate acronym to remind us to HALT. Realize that under these conditions we may be compromised.

Men and testosterone levels when stressed

Men and women both have testosterone in their systems. Yet on average, a man has over 10 times more testosterone in their system than a woman does. Men tend to have more body mass than a woman does. When men get stressed and angry, they pump out way more testosterone. More aggressive, more competitive, more fight, more win, more protect.

All these are strengths - yet during conflict, sometimes one's strengths can become one's weakness. So gentlemen, it is wise to realize when and how you may be a bit more triggered during conflict. These gut instincts may try to take over the strength of your rational thought.

Here is a consideration. If you are in the presence of another man who is really stressed, watch your body language. As a quick tip, do not stand face to face as it may trigger 'Alpha dog'. I don't mean getting into their personal space, as that will definitely trigger something and it won't be good. I just mean a subtle subconscious trigger if you are face to face - man to man smack dab in front of them.

Instead, consider standing slightly turned to the side so the torsos are facing away from each other. Not directly at each other. Your heads may be slightly turned to look at the other in a 'conversational style', not an aggressive 'I'll tell you right to your face' style. Again, we are talking about triggers when stressed so we can be aware and get control.

Women and P. P. P.

P.P.P. stands for Pre-Period Pigout. Now wait a minute. If there are any men thinking about skipping this bit because they don't have periods and it doesn't relate to them, let me ask you this. Do you have any women in your life? Any sisters, mother, aunts, co-workers, friends, cousins, customers, or women in your community? If yes, then is it safe to say that at some point a woman's issue will become a man's issue? Fair enough.

Here's the thing. Just before that time of the month, women tend to have a huge appetite. Her body is getting ready for a potential pregnancy. I remember back in the day when I had periods and here is what I know for sure.

If I've had two breakfasts and three chocolate bars and it's not even noon yet, I'd realize that I must be going through P. P. P.

I'd then realize, that in the next couple of days, I might just be a wee bit more

SENSITIVE !!!

than the rest of the month. And it's smart for me to know that.

The real point I want to make is this. There will be obvious, classic, standard times when we will not be in a good position to handle conflict as rationally, calmly and reasonably as we'd like. Although we may not be super savvy in handling conflict well during those times, we can be capable of recognizing when such times arise. It doesn't serve a purpose to beat yourself up because you didn't handle it well. In future, preempt it by knowing when you will be compromised. It's smart to know when we're stupid.

Now sometimes we may not have the luxury of knowing in advance when we may be compromised in our ability to handle conflict. Sometime we are perfectly fine . . . and then a conflict arises. While it is just starting, we feel everything is starting to go wrong. Fear not, we have a tip for that in the next chapter.

Be sure to check out www.BeforeItHitsTheFan.com to access more tips.

Stop and Stall

This is brilliant! I hope you take advantage of this tip often. It is a fantastic rescue! Here is how you use it.

Anytime you or the other person is getting more upset, stressed, or emotional, stop it from getting worse. It is a way of having some kind of interruption from continuing so you can take some kind of a break. It is designed to protect you and that other person from doing or saying something that can't be taken back.

I repeat with intent, when we are stressed and in conflict, it can be hard to think of the right thing to say. We are temporarily compromised from our ability to think as rationally. It's about being proactive in avoiding something happening that you will regret. If you know you or the other person is getting too stressed, take control before it gets more out of control.

You can do a *Stop and Stall* for 30 seconds when on a heated phone call. You can do a *Stop and Stall* for 24 hours with a colleague at work. If you can do a *Stop and Stall* before it hits the fan, you've done well.

It's like a game of chess - forethought wins. Plant in your arsenal that in those moments, when whatever conflict going on is getting worse, you will consider if a *Stop and Stall* will work about now. Think of it as strategic procrastination.

Sometimes your brain just needs a little time to think of the right thing to say. We all have epiphanies yet they rarely happen when in the heat of the moment. Maybe you need to stop so you can find the time to get the information you need to make an informed decision. Maybe you need to stop to get support from a manager or HR, check with a client, confirm something in the contract, or just to breath and let your brain catch up on what is going on.

Anytime you feel under pressure and you know you don't know what to do or say, *Stop and Stall*. It is hard to think under pressure. Like Captain Kirk did in Star Trek, he changed the rules of the game so he could have an advantage. When the situation seems insane, Stop and Stall. Get out of the game so you can re-group or restrategize before you get back in.

Here is how a Stop and Stall may work during a phone call

Let's say you have a customer on the phone who is really upset. They don't know you, have never met you, and they are heatedly blaming you for what has gone wrong. They are clearly upset and their bad mood is turning ugly. You have every right to feel that righteous indignation. You don't deserve to be treated this way. It is normal that you may start to feel a tad stressed. You know the customer is not always right. Yet you know the customer needs to be treated right. If you get upset or take on a tone that is stressed or fed-up, it may be like throwing gasoline on a fire. Makes it worse.

You want to keep yourself from feeling completely humiliated and spent by the bad mood abuses of a customer and you want to stop the customer from being on a roll with their conflict. Whether the customer has a right to be upset or not, this is about you and how you can handle it when this kind of conflict happens to you.

- Take a deep calming breath of air. Fill your lungs with invisible energy.

- Sit up straight or stand up. Feel tall and empowered.

- Put a gracious smile on your face with your head held high.

- Use the same tone of voice as if you are at the dinner table saying, "Pass the bread, please"

- Then, with your professionally friendly tone of voice and choice of super polite words, say,

"I understand how important it is to resolve this issue for you as soon as possible."

It shows them that you are listening, have prioritized them and their issue as being important, and empathized with how they feel.

Hopefully, that deflates some of their angst

"May I please have permission to put you on a brief 30 second hold while I quickly look into something on your behalf?"

"May I please have permission . . ." is very disarming and extremely polite. Instead of saying, "Let me put you on hold . . ." Maybe they don't want to be put on hold and feel as though again they have no control! It could trigger.

Ere on the side of good manners and politeness

Asking them permission gives them a micro control feeling. Deflates the pent up stress.

". . . to put you on a brief 30 second hold . . " I doubt someone is going to say "Well! Thirty seconds is just too much!!!!!" It is such a short and reasonable request of mere moments. They would almost look silly if they refused. Someone in conflict does not want to lose face. They are not being ignored and it is such a very brief hold.

". . . while I quickly look into something on your behalf." Now you could play with this part a little bit. The goal is for them to feel they and their issue is important and needs to be dealt with. Perhaps you could say "while I ask my manager something on your behalf" This is the higher authority method. It implies that you are putting them on a brief hold while you speak to someone more important on their behalf. May make them feel more special and less defensive.

Once you put them on hold, ensure you put a timer on so at exactly thirty seconds, you pick up the phone and reconnect with them. Don't let them think that your word is not your bond.

Just by showing your integrity of being punctual speaks volumes! Of course you will thank them for being on hold and that you appreciate it. Hopefully during those thirty seconds, they have been able to relax a bit from a lockjaw of conflict. It gives them some time to reflect while they briefly wait.

Now back to you

When you put them on hold, do something immediately to help get rid of your stress. You have thirty full seconds! You can get rid of a lot of stress in that time.

- Throw your arms up in the air a few times in a victory 'Woo-Hoo' stance. Do some kickboxing, jumping jacks, some burst of energy of exercise, punch a piece of paper, do a little jig.

- Have a bite of chocolate, take a smell of that beautiful flower or food item nearby, close your eyes and do a mini meditation, look in a mirror and say to yourself, "I love and accept myself in this moment."

- Remind yourself, "It's not about me." Be the bigger person and visualize the conflict washing off your back like water off a duck. Stress feeds on negative thoughts so think happy.

- Find a way to put a humourous spin on it. Humour instantly jumps you off of the severity of what is going on and helps synapse everything from a different perspective. The laughter will give you a dose of endorphins, dopamine and serotonin.

- Think of music - a particular song that brings a smile or sense of joy. We had rhythm in the womb. Music is magic in how it changes how we humans feel. Sing a song in your head to instantly change the chemicals. Every thought we have secretes certain chemicals in the brain.

You can't control all stress. You can control stress reduction.

Let's say you need to do a longer Stop and Stall with a co-worker.

Perhaps you are in your office with your colleague across the desk from you. Maybe the two of you don't get along that smoothly in the first place. It happens. Sometimes we don't click with every employee. Either way, we must maintain professional relationships and communicate with diplomacy and dignity.

Let's say as you are communicating, you notice your co-worker getting upset, stressed, voice is changing, you can see and feel the stress in their body. Perhaps you are the one feeling stressed or maybe both of you are starting to spiral up in a potential dance of conflict. Take control before it gets out of control. Do a Stop and Stall before it hits the fan

- Take a deep calming breath of air.
- Maintain a respectful, non-threatening body positioning.
- Use the same tone of voice as if you are at the dinner table saying "Pass the bread, please."

"I understand how important it is to resolve this issue in a timely manner. I just need some time to . . .

- Think about it
- Confirm something with my manager
- Check with the client

- Go over the contract or agreement
- Look at both sides

Whatever excuse makes sense and gives you an exit. Maybe you are comfortable to say that you have a personal mandate to not make hasty decisions and that this matter deserves your full attention and due thought.

"May we please reconvene tomorrow morning? Does 9:30 work for you?"

The key is to do this while things are still relatively calm. Preemptive. Have the two of you separated before things get worse. Protect you and the other person from doing or saying something that can't be taken back. Once that person leaves your office, then go directly into "damage control." This means to destress.

Don't let the stress be buried alive to manifest physically and mentally. Get the information you need. Take a break to reflect. Get the support of your boss or others, confirm you know what the facts are, know where you stand and what options are available. When you get home, perhaps relax, play with the kids, do no housework, go out for dinner, enjoy a glass of wine, get a good night sleep. Stress is the #1 killer. Be serious about preventative measures of destressing with intent.

Music is a fast way to instantly reduce stress

There is so much information out there on the powerful effects of music and what it does to the brain and the human spirit. When doing a *Stop and Stall*, music can quickly change everything. The calming effects of 60 baroque music is legendary in how it affects the brain. A few bars of a favorite song can elevate our moods and bring fond memories and feelings bursting forth.

Has it ever happened to you that you get in your car, turn the radio on, and you hear 20 seconds of a song you haven't heard in twenty years. And as the song continues, you find you know every word to this song you haven't heard in twenty years. There you are singing it out word for word verbatim! Even though you hated that song twenty years ago, there you are singing away . . .

It only takes seconds of a tune you hear for you to remember so much more. I bring this up because I really want you to remember the *Stop and Stall* tip. And because I love you all, I want to do something very special for you to ensure you don't forget it. So I have come up with a song. You will be able to hear the song if you go to www.BeforeItHitsTheFan.com as I plan on uploading a new version of it. I will apologize in advance for totally butchering a very fine tune I am using for this song as I am not a singer by trade. Yet it is so valuable to remember this tip that I believe a song will help you remember it.

The Stop and Stall song

You can sing it to yourself now, and then use it (sing it in your head or think of it) when you need to do a *Stop and Stall*.

Any Motown fans out there? I've taken the classic tune, "Stop in the Name of Love" sung by Diana Ross and the Supremes and changed the words.

Here we go:

Start the music . . .

> "Stop, in the Name of Stress
>
> Before you Cause Duress
>
> Think it O - O - ver"

It helps if you do the dance with stop sign gesture.

The B.I.T.C.H. Perspective

Hey Ladies, since we are talking about being assertive communicators, we must address the elephant in the room.

When a man is assertive, he is called **Successful.**

When a woman is assertive, she is called a **Bitch.**

What's with that? Yet more importantly, look what may be holding you back. Sometimes we women worry too much about what people think of us. Some of us fear if we are assertive, then people will call us a Bitch. Is that what may be holding you back from effectively handling conflict?

Don't let it hold you back, let it propel you! Remember, how you perceive something determines how you feel about it, and how you will act on it. What does "bitch" mean to you?

Let's have some fun with this since we girls just want to have fun anyway

Isn't it a dog? Is that such a bad thing? If they are dyslexic, they will be calling you god. And isn't a dog human kind's most valued and faithful companion?

Having the love and affection of a dog is a wonderful thing. They are glad to see you. They live in the moment. They bring dogs into the hospital to bring joy to those suffering, therapy dogs come to the university and colleges during exam times, dogs are brought into courtrooms to help ease the trauma of children testifying. Being called a dog or bitch (a female dog) is sounding pretty noble about now.

Remember, some people will try to silence you by attempting to blame or shame you for being a bitch. Others will respect you for standing up for what you think is right.

**"No one can make you feel
inferior without your consent."**

- Eleanor Roosevelt

**"What other people think of
you is none of your business."**

- Regina Brett

Here are some acronyms for Bitch I think you will appreciate:

Best
Individual
The
Company
Hired

Boys
I'm
Taking
Charge
Here

Being
In
Total
Control
of
Herself

Be
Inspired
To
Change
Habits

Wow, with acronyms like that, one can only hope to be called a Bitch!

Being an assertive, respectful, and diplomatic communicator is worth more than it's weight in gold when it comes to the business world. There has never been a great leader who wasn't a great communicator. Leadership is the most in demand out there and the least in supply because it is tough. Mother Teresa, Princess Diana, Oprah Winfrey, Angela Merkel, Malala Yousafzai, they all stepped right into conflict to bring a peaceful change.

Being a strong communicator is a wonderful thing, ladies. Don't hide your light! Margaret Thatcher had a great quote that may motivate you to realize the power of women. "If you want to get something said, ask a man. If you want to get something done, ask a woman."

Men and women both bring amazing strengths to the table. Don't you forget it (insert a loving yet nagging finger waving in front of you)

www.LornaMcLaren.com

Focus your F.E.A.R.

Just the thought of conflict can create a feeling of fear. The general ambiguous word Fear may conjure up stress and negative premonitions. You lose a sense of control, per se. Fear of the unknown.

Next time you think about or feel any paralyzing effects of Fear, when it comes to conflict resolution, try changing how you perceive it. It gets the brain from panic and high cortisol to a more beneficial way of how you think, feel, and react.

Change your words to change your focus. Different ideas and options come to mind. A different way for the brain to be activated. The brain starts to think in the way you ask of it.

It's like in emergency driver training. If you find yourself losing control of the car, look at where you want to end up and you intuitively/sub consciously place the rudder in that direction and go that way. At least that's the theory. Like learning to ski trees, you look between the trees, not at them. Does "Look down, fall down" ring a bell (or a concussion) to my snowboarding / wakeboarding /sky skiing friends?

It's normal to feel fear communicating in the waters of conflict. Focus on where you want to go. Place the rudder. Have a guiding light. If fear is holding you back, by changing how you focus on fear, you can instantly trigger a more positive and specific process of thought.

Bottom line. If you're going to think about or feel FEAR, focus your F.E.A.R. on one of these options . . .

False Expectations
Appearing Real

Sometimes we assume something to be true when in fact it may be about something else. Perceptions are different, misunderstandings happen. **False Evidence Appearing Real** also falls into this category. Someone at a workshop said the *Spider Man* movie quoted it that way.

Imagine you are asked to introduce yourself to a group of people who you don't know at your first meeting about learning to speak in public. You just came to the meeting. Didn't expect to be called on. Your plan was to just listen in. There are 47 people in the audience. Nothing about them is threatening . . . yet you panic. You are speaking in public! Something apparently feared more than death! Wasn't it Seinfeld who said "We'd rather be in the coffin than giving the eulogy?"

Instead of sitting back and observing a group of people learning, you are now standing in front of everyone! You focus on the fear that everyone is looking at you. You feel the fear of humility. Are they judging how inarticulate you are? Are you sweating under the arms, are your eyes in a panic as you don't know where to look? You completely lose the link from your brain to your mouth. You fear looking like an idiot. You are visualizing them doing the Loser sign with their fingers on their forehead as they cross the street to avoid you. The mere thought of this fear gets your head tingling with the adrenalin. Your body is mildly trembling and you realize you haven't taken a breath in a while. You bail on your speech after 45 seconds and sit down avoiding eye contact with everyone as you try to regain your composure.

When you look up, you are surprised by the support everyone gives you! Some share how they were the same or worse the first time. Some gave such motivating, specific, and positive feedback that you feel good and want to do it again. You hadn't perceived the truth of what was actually going on because of your perceived fear. Completely different reality than you expected.

During conflict, be empathetic to how that person may feel and listen for facts and perceptions. With conflict, sometimes you just need to let them talk.

"One of the best ways to honor someone is to listen to them"

Letting them talk also relieves pent up stress so they can then start to think more rationally. Ever had someone rudely vent to you on the phone then apologize for their behaviour once they got rid of some stress and could think clearly again?

So approach the conflict with the intent to learn if "everyone is on the same page." Is there a misunderstanding? Do we have the same information? Do we know what the facts are? Is there false evidence or false expectations "appearing" real?

Focus on you being a detective to discern if there is false expectations/evidence appearing real.

Another beneficial focus on fear is …

Fail Early and Responsibly

Ignoring a problem in the hopes it will go away is a recipe for disaster. I'm sure we've all been there. Ever worked with a chronically impossible person? Does anyone ever think, "Gosh am I ever glad no one let them know how toxic they are to the rest of the team and that the conflict will only continue to get worse!"

The sooner you learn of the problem, failure or communication breakdown the better. Detect and correct while it is small,

Consider the word "responsible" simply means "able to respond"

If you find out what the problem or misunderstanding is in the infancy state, you are more likely to resolve it. If the conflict is left unchecked, it may grow out of proportion or out of control.

As an example, Fail Early And Responsibly is sage advice when starting a business. Some people have a great idea, start a business, and then lose their shirt when the unexpected occurs and they can't recover from it. Others do a business plan first. They look for what may go wrong in advance and fix it in their business plan before making the mistake in real life. We learn through mistakes.

As a young child, you touch a burning iron; you learn not to do that again. You get burned in a relationship; you learn not to do that again. Some of our greatest lessons come from learning how not to do it. The sooner we learn, the better. Turn your fear into opportunity to learn and grow. Every time we learn something we become more confident and competent.

"There is no problem you can't learn yourself out of!"

So embrace the idea of learning sooner than later where a conflict or misunderstanding is happening. Take responsibility in learning what the conflict is in its infancy state, before it gets out of control.

Now, if it looks like the conflict is going to happen, you can't avoid it, the next F.E.A.R. acronym may help your perspective.

Face Everything
and Recover

A big stressor in life is when we don't have a sense of control. Fear of the unknown. We can't control everything. Sometimes that unexpected conflict or crisis comes out from nowhere and then BAM! Whacks you in the side of the head.

It's normal to want to avoid conflict in fear of not knowing (or having control of) what will happen as a result. It's normal to fear we'll botch it up especially if we have a track record of doing so. It's not uncommon to fear it may get worse, fear failure, fear we may not know how to handle it in the moment. It's normal to have self-doubt. Yet sometimes we forget how capable we really are.

I'll bet you are far more capable than you give yourself credit for. Sometimes we humans are our own worst critics. We all struggle with self-esteem issues somehow someway. Some of us struggle more than others. Some of us struggle more at particular times or during certain events in our lives. I personally believe low self-esteem is one of the most crippling diseases out there!

When we don't feel confident in ourselves, we question and doubt our abilities. Sometimes we focus on what we don't do well more than what we are good at. We may project an expectation of failure.

It's like being asked, "What is your greatest weakness?" If you are like the way I used to be, you could go on for days about what you are not good at. Yet when asked, "What is your greatest strength?" Do you find you are a tad speechless, not sure what to say? Your positive list is nowhere near as long as your weakness list?

Some are so wired to acknowledge others strengths yet put themselves on the back burner. Do you have no problem giving someone a compliment, yet struggle accepting one yourself? Do you have compassion for others, yet little for yourself? Hmmm, sounding like a double standard.

The point I want to make is that sometimes we forget how very capable we are. Think back on all the crap you've been through already in your life! I'll bet you've gone through some tough times in your past yet made it through. Do you laugh and have joy in your life today even though you went through challenging times in the past? You handled it, survived it; perhaps you became stronger as a result. Maybe you have a new awareness or new found purpose and appreciation for life as a benefit?

Believe in yourself. You are capable. You have been capable in the past and you will be capable again to handle what comes your way. You can't control everything. Just face it and focus on the goal of a successful recovery. A sense of hope and belief is a positive human motivator. Look between the trees, not at them. Let your goal pull you through. The brain doesn't visualize "don't" so be aware of the words you are using.

Know that you can face it and recover. You have a bunch of tips to help you through conflict. One small step in conflict and stress reduction - one big step to a happier you.

Be sure to check out **www.BeforeItHitsTheFan.com** to access more tips.

And if all else fails . .

F Everything and Run

It's important to recognize when *it's just too much!*

Seriously, this is wise advice. Sometimes you are not in a position to handle the conflict. Perhaps it's too overwhelming, too hurtful and the emotions are so close to the surface. Or, you are so very deeply involved or isolated, you can't see straight or objectively. Maybe no one understands you, you feel so alone in the situation, you don't have any support from others. These are all good reasons to consider avoiding conflict resolution until you can look after yourself first. Put your oxygen mask on first.

People cut their losses all the time in other areas; business ventures, investments, relationships. It is good to know when it is not worth it to even go there with certain conflict. Unfortunately, I hear this in the business world too often. Highly capable people, strong work ethic, proud to work hard for the success of the company they work for end up leaving this way. It often happens to good people and to good companies. It is tragic. Yet not really surprising.

It is no secret that one of the top reasons someone chooses to leave a job is because of unresolved conflict with someone else. They share their stories with me. You'd be amazed what I hear from the years of working with so many professionals in personal and professional development events. It is when they realize a certain conflict, toxic person, or unresolved situation will not change. Some people put up with an unresolved conflict for many years until the health and stress of it all takes away from their quality of life. Or the company has employees "retired at their desks." They have left, albeit not physically.

Conflict is costly. To ignore it even more so

How does not knowing how to handle basic necessities of life set us up for success? Think about it, how many of us were really prepared for life after high school? Did you understand credit cards and how they work? Loans, debt, or how to pay off debts? What to do with money once you have it, how to make investments? Could you explain compound interest or how to prepare and do your income tax? Did you learn any entrepreneurial skills? Critical thinking skills? Working with others and group problem solving? Did that prepare you for making a livelihood?

Were you prepared going into the workforce? Have you ever had a job where they didn't give you a job description? They didn't have the time to train you? You were not clear on how to determine a priority so you waste valuable time doing something that didn't need to be done in the first place? No one gives you feedback or coaching? Did you learn the skills on how to communicate and work in a team of diverse individuals? If not taught or shown how to communicate with diplomacy, clarity, and manage conflict in a work environment then it is no surprise at some point, it will get out of control. It is a fact that when 1st aid and safety awareness is taught, accidents go down.

Unresolved interpersonal conflict in the workplace is one of the largest reasons for lost productivity, low morale, and loss of good employees and customers. It's a tough one to address. Most people are not comfortable with conflict and avoid it to their peril. According to the National Institute for Occupational Safety, the stress of Interpersonal conflict on the job is one of the top causes for reducing worker health.

Personal issues may fall under this F.E. And Run category as well

Difficult conversations and uncomfortable topics were not discussed in our home. I remember a time feeling devastated due to personal tragedy. I couldn't function very well in other areas of my life. We had two deaths in the immediate family in less than two years shortly after graduating from high school. Ian and I were close. Dad and I had a special bond. I was out of town when each of them died. Don't know if you ever come to terms with a suicide and it was so shocking dad's fatal heart attack in his mid-50's. One felt broken. The stressed workaholic father died of a broken heart. I was going to school in Guadalajara, Mexico when Ian died. He was planing on coming down to join me. Instead I came home as if in a surreal dream. No one knew what to say, so we didn't. We dealt with it individually.

I threw myself into full time work, school in the evenings, partying with friends, and trying to find joyful purpose and blissful avoidance. Living in an apartment away from the pain in the eyes of our family in shell shock helped. The 'difficult' topic was not addressed, or worked through with discussion. Stiff upper lip. We didn't have the tools or practice to discuss such a conflictual topic.

Carry on we did. Ignore the conflict, It will go away . . .

By getting away, moving into a different environment, immersing myself in work and school, I made myself busy with some kind of purpose. It helped to avoid the pain. I did not properly address or work through Ian's death so that when dad died, another piece of my heart and world shattered, as did a sense of stability to life.

I feared my own depression and questioned my sense of purpose to my life. I did a "F Everything And

Run." At the age of 20, I jumped on a plane and left the continent. I thought if I put myself in a foreign country where I have to learn a new language, learn to find a job and survive, get away from all this, I won't have time to think about my misery at home. I needed a change in my life, et voila.

I ended up in France. I knew no one there, could speak a bit of Spanish, not French. Skied four winters in the Alps of Val D'Isere to heal my heart. Learned the language working in restaurants. Spent the summers working in either Paris or the Cote D'Azure! I don't know how I would have survived if I hadn't gotten away to heal, find perspective, and new goals. What an amazing country to go to to learn different perspectives in from age 20 to 25!!! I will forever be grateful for the life altering experience and positive turn to my life as a result of my time in France. Merci! I was renewed! Came home to Canada.

Of course when you are older with commit-ments, it's not as easy to simply run away. Yet please realize when it is too much for you to handle. Take some time for yourself. You can't control all stress, you can control stress reduction (I repeat with intent).

Please know I have heard my share of tragic and sad situations with the stress of unresolved conflict in the workplace. This is what I do for a living. People get physically ill from the constant stress of it all and share their stories with me. The number one killer is stress.

Get out of a bad situation before it takes you out.

Cut your losses and leave. Run. Do some "Woo-hoos!" between breaths.

Q.T.I.P.

Quit
Taking
It
Personally

How we perceive things determines how we feel. Sometimes we take things personally when it doesn't necessarily have anything to do with us. It's normal. It is also a habit that takes practice to break if you have detrimental triggers with this. Sometimes if someone is rude to you, you think, "What did I do to deserve this?" Maybe you did diddly squat! Maybe they are just a rude person!

Stress feeds on negative thoughts so to help you during conflict, visualize yourself stepping out of the frying pan of blame or any ill will. Force yourself to see it from a different perspective.

When we witness or experience something, we have that little voice in our head that tells us in a millisecond how to perceive the situation. Be aware of what it is telling you when you start to feel conflict and some angst or defensiveness in your veins. The Q.T.I.P. can come in handy to keep conflict from arising on your end.

Here is an example of how you can use it.

Let's say you are speaking at a meeting with about 30 people. You've prepared, it is all really important information, and it is your job to initiate this change with your employees. While you are speaking, you notice someone at the back doing huge yawns. You find it very distracting. Of course if everyone in the room is yawning, then you are the common denominator. Yet when just the one person does, if we are in a weakened state of ego or low self esteem, that little voice in your head starts to go off on a tangent of taking it personally.

In a millisecond, your brain is saying, "Boy is that person ever rude. Here I am doing my job and it is important while we pay you to be here to learn this stuff. Obviously it is distracting seeing you blatantly show no respect for me and what I am doing for the success of our company as you yawn away. Oh look, that person now has their hand up. They have a question for me? Well, they have been so rude to me that I'm just going to ignore them. They can figure it out themselves since they yawned through my presentation."

Where is your logic going? Down the toilet! Maybe it has nothing to do with you.

Whether they mean to personally insult you or not, I'm just saying, 'Don't take it personally'. We all have an ego. Sometime we've just got to say to ourselves, "Let go of my ego."

Or, if we are struggling with low self esteem issues, we perceive the yawns in a different way. That little voice in our head goes, "Oh no, I am boring them to death. What a bad speaker I am. What made me think I could do this in the first place, I'll probably put everyone to sleep. I better get a new job." Of course I am taking it a bit to an extreme to make a point.

If you find yourself taking it personally, force yourself to see it from a different perspective. Here is a fact. You don't have a gun to their head making them yawn. They don't have a gun to your head making you take it personally. All you know for sure is that they are yawning.

Maybe they worked a graveyard shift. Maybe they have a colicky baby at home. Maybe they were out all night dancing to "Stop in the Name of Stress." Have you ever tried yoga? Isn't it true that in yoga, people take deep breaths of air with intent to oxygenate the system? Why yes it is true. Maybe they are just doing yoga and it has nothing to do with you! Maybe they are so tired yet so interested in what you have to say that they are yawning to stay awake and not miss a word!

Let's say that person is now closing their eyes and it looks like they are asleep. That little voice in our head could go, "How rude they are. How dare they do this to me." If there is only one person that seems in conflict with what you are doing, we sometimes focus on the negative and ignore all the other positive things going on. Don't take it personally.

Focus on your job, your goal, your agenda and be aware to not let it get to you. A healthy sense of self esteem is important. When we feel good about ourselves, we are less likely to be defensive, take it personally, cry, yell, or disengage.

We all have triggers, we want to feel accepted, we don't want to lose face, we don't want to feel ostracized or unappreciated. If you feel a trigger bringing you and your self esteem down, stop taking it personally and find a different way of perceiving it.

When you have internal conflict, just make up a reason for them having their eyes closed that makes you feel good. Pretend the reason that person's eyes are closed is because they are visualizing your every word. Now how do you feel?

In the words of James Brown, "Whoa! I feel good, do-do, do-do, do-do, do"

It is better to have the brain work towards a positive goal than to be derailed by a perception and direction of conflict.

I am always blown away by the creativeness and resourcefulness of the people I meet. I remember coming back to a company for a second training event a few months after I had first worked with them. I was welcomed with huge smiles and asked to see if I noticed anything new. There were the most curious and interesting artsy flowers in a pot on the counter between them and their customers. It was actually Q-tips with the tips painted yellow and the stem painted green all arranged in a cute little pot. Adorable! And what a great idea for a subtle reminder!

At another event, I showed the participants pictures of these yellow Q.t.i.p. flowers. They loved it! One woman said she was going to do something similar. She promised to send me a photo. Sure enough, I was again so delightfully impressed. She had colorful Q Tips with tiny leaves and petals as if they were an array of numerous flowers in a bunch of little pots. These lovely displays of Q.t.i.p. flowers where throughout the office.

Consider having a Q.t.i.p. nonchalantly beside everyone's phone to remind them to not take it personally if they spend most of their day on the phone. It takes determination to be aware and to change a habit. Repetition is the mother of learning. Having reminders and practice works wonders.

The joyous coloured flowers and healing natural green leaves puts such a positive spin on **Quit Taking**

It Personally. If you come up with a way to incorporate the Q.T.I.P. in your environment, please do me the honour and great joy of sending me a picture. I'd love to see it!

Be sure to check out www.BeforeItHitsTheFan.com to access more tips.

Just Do Your Best
and Flush the Rest

Whoever came up with this quote is a genius! Oh such sage advice! Look, you are not going to be perfect. If you are a perfectionist, you've chosen an unattainable goal! We learn through our mistakes. Some of our most powerful lessons we learned through a mistake. Even that children's book series "The Berenstein Bears." The whole objective and success of those books were to learn from the mistakes the endearing dad made.

We kids growing up enjoyed many British shows that showed conflict laced with laughter. It was a great outlet for us because we were not taught how to address or manage conflict. Our parents meant well, and the rule was to respect your elders no matter what, sweep any conflict under the carpet, don't bring up a conflictual conversation as it is rude. Instead be quiet, polite and have a stiff upper lip. Felt as if we were wrong, rude, or bad to acknowledge or discuss a conflict.

Fawlty Towers with John Cleese playing Basil Fawlty was one of our favorite shows. You'd laugh and learn by watching how inept he was at his job. Did you know that John Cleese used to do Management Training Videos?

In my mid-30's I was trying to get back on my feet after a devastating divorce, shocking business crash alone with a 3 and a 5 year old. I was now a solo-parent working full time at a low paying job away from my hometown and family. Again my self-esteem was thrown. I needed to better myself to provide for my children.

Our parents taught us to be self-sufficient, not complain, and not ask for financial help. I'd been working since age 15, moved out of the house in my teens, and left my hometown of Vancouver for many years. Although it was hard, I was proud of getting through this difficult time without complaining to my family or asking for help. No one wants to be the embarrassment to the family. Mother was always so concerned about what people would think of her. Couldn't afford it anyway so that was an obvious part of the decision. Vancouver is an expensive place.

Invested any little money I had into professional training and development. Yet I felt thwarted. While taking night courses at the college on Management Training, we had an instructor who would fill the overhead projector screen with information, and then read it to us for the next two hours!

Not to brag, yet all of us in that room knew how to read! It felt like cheating to have a teacher read to us. It begged the question, "What was the point of having a teacher there?"I resented spending my hard earned money on a night school course with someone who didn't know how to teach. Yet the best part was when he put on the John Cleese Management Training videos. We howled with laughter watching the mistakes while simultaneously learning instantly how to correct them. Humour has always been a saviour when it comes to conflict and challenges. It's healthy not to take things too seriously. Humour is also one of the fastest ways of reducing stress.

In the beginning of the book, we'd discussed the effects of working with a toxic person who no one addresses about conflict resolution. A toxic person can wipe out an organization of it's good employees. Someone with a high level of dignity is not going to stay in a toxic environment for long. After leaving a job that I loved and was very good at, I decided to learn how to become an entrepreneur before starting a second business. The experience with this toxic person took its toll. I wanted to avoid being in another work environment where the manager or higher-up does not know how, or chooses not to, address conflict. More importantly,

I didn't ever want to be in that position again!

My mission was to learn how to communicate effectively especially when it comes to conflict. Unresolved conflict that was ignored or avoided destroyed my family, my marriage, my business, a job I liked, and threatened my self worth.

Back on track

In this entrepreneurial course, they showed us a list of the top 20 wealthiest Americans. Most of them had been fired, gone bankrupt, and/or didn't finish formal college. Some who come to mind are Steve Jobs of Apple, Larry Ellison of Oracle, Walt Disney of Disneyland, Colonel Sanders of KFC. I remember thinking "Wow, I've also been through some of these same devastating setbacks. Woo-Hoo, I must be on the road to success!"

Conflict and things going wrong happens!

You can choose how you will perceive it, feel about it, and act on it. Even when you are doing something enjoyable like camping - there are still mosquitoes, "bzzzz, bzzz, bzz trying to eat you alive." Can't avoid all conflict. Not everyone will like you no matter how wonderful you are. After doing a two hour presentation to 300 women on how to negotiate for more money, I had one woman rate me 1 out of 10. While thinking, what can I learn from this, I read her reasoning behind the low rating. It was because I wasn't wearing enough make-up. I'm not teaching Mary Kay!!! Who cares about whether I am wearing makeup or not! Whether you deserve it or not, there will always be conflict. Just do your best and flush the rest.

Don't be so hard on yourself as you learn your way through conflict resolution. The fact that you are trying in good conscience to resolve conflict is commendable! Look yourself in the mirror while reflecting back on how you handled a conflict. Were you respectful, objective, used facts, and specific so as to reduce misunderstandings and ensure clarity? Were you honest and truthful? If the answer is yes, then you can be proud of yourself.

You are responsible for how YOU act. You are not completely responsible nor can you always control how others will react. They may choose to take it personally as an attack; especially if they are struggling with low self-esteem or misinterpretation of what you meant to say. They may choose to not acknowledge their actions and instead externalize it and blame someone else. They may choose to get angry or highly emotional in the hopes that you won't want to bring it up again. They may be passive-aggressive and get you back in some way that makes no sense. Just do your best and flush the rest. Let it go! Consider it a process of elimination . . .

If we avoid or say nothing about a conflict, we show a form of false advertising - basically giving them permission to continue with the conflictual behaviour. Silence is acceptance.

Resolving conflict is one of the top three high-leverage activities in a work environment according to Dr. Stephen R. Covey.

Anytime you spend in acknowledging and resolving conflict, the return on that valuable time investment comes back a hundredfold! Covey's work has withheld the test of time. By learning how and practicing conflict resolution is an admirable investment. It is a commendable character strength.

Release perfectionism. You'll never be perfect. Think about it, if you are trying to reach an impossible and unrealistic goal of perfection, how motivating does it feel to be a loser every day that you don't succeed? I'm serving sarcasm (out of love) to make a point. We often learn our most valuable lessons through our mistakes!

People don't like perfect people anyway. I remember being on a flight where someone gave me one of those trash Hollywood magazines to flip through. When you are looking at that perfect, famous, life is easy person, don't you just feel like giving them a little flick off that pedestal? And then there are those perfectionist who never get anything done!

Embrace being human. Make and learn through the mistakes. Don't try to be perfect. You can't be perfect and we won't like you anyway. We are constantly being educated by our own experience.

Learn, reflect, and let go.

It does not serve a purpose "beating yourself up" about how you did or didn't handle a particular conflict. Practice makes improvement. I'm a strong downhill skier. Have spent years on ski hills and had my fill of bailing or losing control, crashing, getting up and doing it again with the powerful skill of learning "how not to do it" next time. It's all in the recovery. The more you practice, the faster you recover from mistakes, or the faster you learn to avoid making the same mistake next time.

Your intention is paramount. If your intention is to address and resolve conflict with respect and appreciation for our differences, you are more likely to succeed. If your intention is to follow a particular spiritual path, you are more likely to make decisions that honour that spiritual path. Your intention can be like a guiding light. If your focus is fear, avoidance, assumption of doing things wrong and making it worse during conflict, your thoughts and actions may be engaged in leading you to that destination.

During conflict, if your intention is to do your best, you subconsciously follow that path. Focus on what you want to have happen. Don't focus on what you don't want to have happen, as that would be the same as negative goal planning.

Don't beat yourself up! Do your best and flush the rest. The more we harbor guilt, stress, bad-self talk and self-resentment the worse we feel about ourselves. Stress is the #1 killer! Gotta let go of the stress. Don't let the stress kill you from within.Whatever happens in your world, you're in it! You matter! Low self-esteem equals low productivity. How you feel about yourself has a direct impact on how you perceive things and how you act on them.

Doing your best is a noble and worthy intention. Letting go of stress and self-deprecating thoughts is healthy. Being assertive in learning how to communicate with diplomacy and how to manage and resolve conflict is a powerful and important life skill in building relationships. You are an important component to every relationship you have. You can't control all conflict and stress. You can control stress reduction and you can have a direct effect on how conflict is resolved.

When it comes to conflict resolution . . .

Just do your best and flush the rest

Check out **www.BeforeItHitsTheFan.com** to access more tips.

About The Author

Lorna McLaren is an award winning Corporate Trainer and International Speaker in Effective Communication, Conflict Resolution, and Stress Reduction. She's helped thousands of teams, companies, and individuals throughout 7 countries positively change the impact of how they communicate! Enjoy results, reduce stress, and find the funny in our faults.

Lorna has been quoted in various newspapers and magazines such as the "Lawyer's Weekly" on how to best communicate with Power Points, "The Glass Hammer" for Women in Business, "First for Women" and "Hitched" on building better relationships, and "Cosmopolitan Magazine" on the topic "Why Some Men Prefer to Date a Bitch". Being able to communicate with confidence, impact, credibility and diplomacy in many areas of our lives is a skill she loves to teach.

Born and raised in Vancouver, Lorna has lived and worked in Mexico, over 4 years in France, and raised her sons in Kelowna, BC. She has been a promoter, 1st aid instructor, and volunteer patroller with the Canadian Ski Patrol System. She has raised money for the SPCA and awareness of the Pets and People Visiting Society through K9 Frisbee dog events.

As a corporate trainer and speaker, Lorna has spoken at thousands of events with managers, support staff, teams, and entrepreneurs, throughout Canada, USA, England, Scotland, Ireland, Australia, New Zealand, and Tasmania. She has worked with small businesses and Fortune 500 corporations.

Producer of the 5 minute audio Podcast series, "Quick Communication Tips." These tips are designed to help busy professionals master the moment, no matter what hits the fan. All episodes were featured in the top 500 "Movers and Shakers" list.

Learning how to become a dynamic trainer has been a passion of hers. Lorna believes she doesn't have a right to teach if she is not continually upgrading her skills. She has invested much time and zeal in learning how to teach in a way that increases people's energy, keeps them riveted, has a direct positive impact, and motivates people to make changes as they walk out the door.

Most people dread going into an all day training event until they meet Lorna. She will share with you quick tips on how to accelerate your ability to retain information in any learning environment. You can benefit from using the same techniques to be more effective in sharing information and motivating others. Fast, fun, and focused is her training style.

Lorna resides in Vancouver, BC. Being able to spend time in the forest, inline skating the seawall, skiing the trees, bobbing in an ocean, walking anywhere, hanging with friends and family, and being a recipient of really good food gives her much joy!

- Facebook:
  https://www.facebook.com/lorna.mclaren
- LinkedIn:
  https://www.linkedin.com/in/lorna-mclaren
- Amazon Author Page:
  https://www.amazon.com/Lorna-McLaren
- Website: **www.LornaMcLaren.com**
- More tips: **www.BeforeIt HitsTheFan.com**

Hire Lorna To Speak at Your Event!

Book Lorna as your Keynote Speaker and for your Conference breakout sessions!

Bring Lorna in for customized Onsite Training at your Company!

You're Guaranteed to Make Your Event Highly Engaging and Memorable with Positive Results!

For more info, visit
www.LornaMcLaren.com

or call +1 (778) 879-2120 PST

Or email:
Lorna@McLarenFormulaTraining.com

IF you liked this book ...

I really hope you enjoyed this book and found it useful. If so, I'd be very grateful if you'd post a short review on Amazon. Your support really does make a difference and I really appreciate it :)

If you noticed any spelling mistakes, I'd be most appreciative if you'd give me a heads up on what page. If you recognize who said a particular quote, or have a story you'd like to share, let me know.

Thanks again for your support!

Free book updates and training tips

To get updates of this book, free training videos and audio tips, visit:

www.BeforeItHitsTheFan.com

www.ingramcontent.com/pod-product-compliance
Lightning Source LLC
Chambersburg PA
CBHW070728220326
41598CB00024BA/3349